Praise for
Releasing the Butterfly

Once into Releasing the Butterfly, I could not put it down.

A remarkable story — a love story, a career and family story, a health story, a tragedy, and an inspiring source of wisdom and comfort for us all, no matter what our circumstances are. It is likely the case that each reader will find his or her struggles in the account of Max and Gene Alice's lives together. The joy, the pain, the hard times, the fun are all part of our lives and Max Sherman shows how one leads to another and then back again. He mixes despair with hope and love and acceptance so beautifully.

— **Susan Beresford,** former President of the Ford Foundation

Releasing the Butterfly is so honest, it hurts. However, it may help someone else groping fearfully down that dark corridor.

— **Bill Moyers,** journalist

In Max Sherman's beautiful book we are given not only a vivid and indelible portrait of a talented, resolute, and fiercely independent woman, but also a memorable journey, by turns joyous, devastating, instructive, and inspiring. The description of the powerful partnership that sustained Max and Gene Alice through this journey will claim a permanent place in the reader's mind and heart.

— **Esther Mackintosh,** President Emeritus of the
Federation of State Humanities Councils

Music and especially Sacred Music has always been important to Gene Alice. Any proceeds from this little book will go to Austin Presbyterian Theological Seminary's program in sacred music.

Releasing the
Butterfly

Developmental Editor: Mary Ann Roser
Cover Design by Heidi Dorey
Interior Design by Danielle H. Acee, authorsassistant.com

ISBN: 978-0-578-78487-8
Cataloging-in-Publication Data
Sherman, Max
Releasing the Butterfly/Max Sherman
p. cm.
Library of Congress Control Number: 2020920437

First edition 2020.

Releasing the
Butterfly

A Love Affair in Four Acts

A Memoir by
Max Sherman

For Gene Alice, the love of my life

ACT I

Chapter One

I love a low-key evening. No excitement, no surprises. That's the kind of evening Gene Alice and I were having when it took an unexpected turn. I did not see it coming, perhaps because the evening had unfolded in the most spectacularly ordinary way.

We were in the apartment and had just watched a re-run of *Mission Impossible*, one of our favorite old-time TV shows, running in syndication. I had slipped off my shoes, exposing a new pair of yellow-and-blue argyle socks. They were loud, but they will make Gene Alice smile, I thought. And she did when she glanced over at them.

Red-stained napkins and plates holding pizza crust still sat on the table, the remains of a simple but tasty dinner. I didn't care about the mess. We were nestled in a pair of recliners in the living room, side by side, close enough that we could clink our wine goblets. We were enjoying a robust Chianti, a Classico Gran Selezione. It was perfect. I wanted to make Gene Alice happy, and when the wine expert steered me to this bottle in his shop, I probably spent a little too much. But Gene Alice always said she wanted a "good Chianti" with her pizza, and, I told myself, she was worth the splurge.

I looked over at her, relaxing in her chair, feet up, the pale blue light of the TV illuminating her delicate profile. It was nearly midnight, and I was tired. The dishes can wait, I told myself. I stood and looked back at Gene Alice. "Let me put the dishes in the sink," I said. "And then let's go to bed." The words were hardly out of my mouth when Gene Alice jumped up and glared at me in fury. She opened her mouth, and I could see her teeth as she started shouting. My first thought was of a lion that had once locked eyes on me before emitting a startling roar at a zoo in Colorado. Then shock. And fear.

"You are not my husband," she screamed. "You have to leave right now. If you don't, I will call the police. I want you to get the hell out of my house, right now!"

She dashed to the door and unlocked it. I ran to her, my mind racing as fast as my heart was thumping. What had set her off? Was it the mention of bed? Was she going to push me out the door or run out instead? I reached for her arm, but she flung me off. She opened the door a few inches. I managed to slam it shut before she could escape. She then tried to push me away with her leg, and I watched in growing astonishment as she summoned the strength of that mother who lifted a car pinning her small child. Gene Alice was determined to get away from me.

This is dangerous and can't happen again, I told myself. Perhaps I had been living in denial, too willing to suppress warning signs that arrived like a flash flood but quickly receded. I realized now I was up to my knees in uncharted waters, and they were drawing me in, deeper and deeper. Clearly, it was time to act, maybe even past time. I made a plan, executed it, and unwittingly set the stage for the awful accident that would change everything. It came just a few nights later in the exact spot where Gene Alice and I had scuffled. I was reduced to lying on the floor of the apartment, writhing in pain, and asking myself: How did we get to this sad, scary place?

Chapter Two

I met Gene Alice at the Hutchinson County Jail in 1953. The jail is in Stinnett, which is in the Texas Panhandle, about fifty-five miles from the Oklahoma border and fifteen miles from Phillips, the town where I grew up.

I was the child of a single mother, Eva Davenport Sherman, whose husband divorced her midway through her pregnancy with me. I don't think he even noticed she was carrying me; I am not mentioned at all in the divorce decree. My father took my five-year-old sister, Billie, to live with him, and when I was just two weeks old, my mom carried me away from the hills of Viola, Arkansas, to the flat oil patch of West Texas. She already had family in Hutchinson County. Her three surviving sisters were brought there by their great-aunt Mary and great-uncle J. O., who raised them. Mom's family toiled as grocers and store owners. Like them, we arrived dreaming of a life better than the hardscrabble existence that had defined the Davenport family's time in the Ozarks. Uncle J. O. was probably the wealthiest man in town, before he let drink and gambling become his boss.

Phillips was in what would be considered a godforsaken scab on the high plains but for the 1921 discovery of oil and gas in Hutchinson County. In fact, the entire Texas Panhandle would not have had a city or a large town had it not been for the petroleum bonanza that started a decade before our arrival. Before oil, those expansive plains were populated by cowboys and the few merchants who supplied agricultural and other goods to the sprawling ranches and their occupants. The new oil and gas economy changed everything. It birthed the first railroads, which proved to be the salvation of the cattle industry as it opened up a national market for beef. It also attracted waves of newcomers, many of whom were down on their luck, like Mom and me.

Our adopted county had been primed for a boom. By 1926, the population of Hutchinson County's new town of Borger was estimated to be between 40,000 and 50,000. The vast majority of its residents lived in tents and shacks spread over the rough, unforgiving landscape, pocked by a few barren hills and crooked crevasses. But opportunity permeated the town and fed everyone's ambitions. Almost overnight, Borger had become home to oilmen, prospectors, roughnecks, panhandlers, fortune seekers, card sharks, bootleggers, prostitutes, and dope peddlers. Not surprisingly, the town's somewhat seedy reputation also made it a haven for criminals and fugitives. Before long, the town government was firmly in the hands of an organized crime syndicate. The Texas Rangers were called in to bring order.

Gene Alice was from Borger.

By today's standards, the less-exciting town of Phillips might have been a prime example of industrial socialism. Everyone lived in a company house. Everyone had a job with Phillips Petroleum Company. Everyone was white. The company owned the hospital, and the doctors were company employees. The public school had one taxpayer, Phillips Petroleum.

As a Phillips student, I never had to pay for anything. If the band needed a new oboe, petroleum tax dollars bought it. If our winning football team needed new helmets or uniforms, which it did when I was on the roster, plenty of industry-supplied tax money sat in the school system's coffers, waiting to be spent. The Phillips High School Field House had the first whirlpool and electric stimulating equipment for sports injuries of any high school in Texas, and quite likely, before any college in the state. Teachers made almost 30 percent more than others in the region because the money was there. And, let's face it, the dry, windswept plains were not a pleasant place to put down stakes. The oil boom made the town more upper class.

My mother taught school in Arkansas, but her credential didn't qualify her to teach in Texas. She needed money now and decided she could make a healthy living by operating a beauty salon. That also was not without sacrifice. Mom had to take a fifty-mile trip to Amarillo every Sunday night to attend the region's only beauty school. Late on Fridays, she would return home where we lived with her oldest sister, my aunt Ann. My aunt and I shared the same birthdate, January 19, and she was a kindly surrogate mother during the week. She worked as a check-out clerk in a grocery store and was married to Jonsie, but that marriage was on life support, and he was not around for long. They had no children, nor did my other aunts.

After Mom graduated from beauty school, she opened Eva's Beauty Shop on Main Street in Old Phillips, which had been named Whittenburg before the oil boom. My great-uncle Walter Goodwin owned almost every building in Old Phillips.

With my mother's new-found financial independence, she and I moved into a one-room stucco shack with a tiny kitchen and a concrete shower. She worked all the time, fixing other women's hair in her beauty shop and cleaning our small home in the few spare moments she had. Going to church did not become a habit for her until long after I left home. But Mom was religious in the faith of her fathers, distinctly Southern Baptist. When I was a baby, she would hold me in her arms as we went to bed and teach me to pray. "Now I lay me down to sleep, I pray the Lord my soul to keep. If I should die before I wake, I pray the Lord my soul to take." That was my first class in theology.

Mom slept on a double bed in the corner by the shower. I slept on a cot near the front door. When I was four, Billie came to live with us after the father I never knew died from injuries he suffered in a car wreck. Our little house was spartan, but it was blessed, literally, because it sat in the shadow of Phillips Southern Baptist Church, a huge influence on my childhood and adolescence. Aunt Ann was the one who taught me to not ever miss Sunday school. When we lived with her, she scrubbed me, dressed me in my finest clothes, and ushered me through the wire gate into the alley and off to church. I did not miss a single Sunday of that routine through my first grade in public school, after which I continued the tradition on my own in the little house Mom and I shared. As an eight-year-old, I qualified for the "Perfect Attendance Bible," given to those who never missed Sunday school.

Just before my twelfth birthday, I gained a wonderful stepfather, John Crupper. We lived with him in an 800-square-foot Phillips company house for a little less than six years, when he tragically died of a heart attack. Death was a part of my life from an early age, but my faith assured me we would one day meet again.

Religious faith was the reason I was at the jail the day I crossed paths with Gene Alice Wienbroer. I was one of four high school boys who held a church service every Sunday afternoon at the jail. I officiated, carrying with me the perfect-attendance Bible I had earned. Everyone at the jail called me Pastor Max, which is funny, because I wasn't really a pastor. I was barely eighteen and had been running the service for nearly two years.

On this momentous Sunday, we invited a quartet of guy friends to sing during the service. They brought a beautiful fifteen-year-old girl to accompany them on an old army fold-up field organ. As she was working to unfold it, I noticed her elegant ankles. She was wearing a long skirt patterned with soft yellow horses and light-pink flowers. When she sat, the skirt dipped down to her lower calves revealing a lovely patch of alabaster. Unlike most of the girls in my high school, she wore leather loafers without white ankle socks. She did not need any embellishment. My eyes were immediately drawn to the smooth skin just above her proper loafers. Her finely chiseled ankles were a work of art.

Gene Alice's loosely curled auburn hair, accented by notes of ginger, framed her radiant face. My heart skipped a beat when she tilted her head to smile at me. I noticed then she was still struggling to unfold the organ.

Instinctively, I asked, "May I help you?"

"No thank you," came the quick reply. "I can do it myself."

Chapter Three

The church, the Bible, and the reverent but sometimes boisterous congregations of the Southern Baptist, Methodist, Church of Christ, and Church of the Nazarene were woven into the fabric of West Texas community life, especially in the Panhandle. Most, if not all, of the kids grew up in the church. For some, it was a religious sanctuary. For others, it was a social hub, akin to Friday night football and making out. For me and for Gene Alice, it was both.

We were alone as she tugged at the organ that Sunday morning. The singers had gone off to another room to warm up their voices. One of the instrument's latches would not give way. Gene Alice was frustrated and looked over at me several times as I was going over my speaking notes. Finally, she surrendered. "Would you help me? I can't get this rusty latch to open."

I happily walked over, eager to be her hero. I attempted to force the latch, but it would not budge. "It needs oil," I told her. "I bet the jailer has a can." I found myself standing shoulder to shoulder with one of the most beautiful girls I had ever seen. She smelled good. It wasn't perfume, just the smell of her clean skin. Thank God for that rusty latch, I thought. Together we strolled down a long hall to the jailer's office. He and I had become friends.

I had inherited the jail service when two older preacher boys from my high school headed off to college. He produced a small can of oil and held it out to me. On the walk back, Gene Alice and I introduced ourselves. She told me about toting that old military field organ to churches across the Panhandle to accompany the quartet. The foursome was a "mixed" group: two Nazarenes, two Baptists. Gene Alice's grandfather was a Southern Baptist minister. There was a note of exasperation in her voice when she said, "Every time the church door opens at Calvary Baptist Church, I am there. Because I play the piano and the organ and because my grandfather is the preacher, I show up to accompany the choir or a soloist. But I can assure you, I have never been to a jail service and I've never performed in front of an audience of men accused of crimes."

I told her I had been recruited to join the jail service because I had a car. My stepfather had loved cars and let me drive his before I was sixteen. When he and my mother married, he drove an old Mercury, but his dream was to own a Lincoln Continental. Five years into the marriage, he got his Lincoln. Four months later, his heart gave out, and he was dead. My mother did not drive, which wasn't all that unusual back in the 1950s. So, the Lincoln was all mine. But with John gone, Mom and I had to move out of our company-owned house. She used the life insurance payout to buy a home in Borger, two miles from where we were living. It had an apartment over a two-car garage. She converted the outside car space into a home beauty salon. I drove back and forth to Phillips in the Lincoln so I could graduate from my high school.

Because Gene Alice was new to the jail, I briefed her on the men on the other side of the bars. Some were doing time for breaking and entering, selling small amounts of marijuana, taking an unlocked car for a joyride, and other assorted, mostly petty, crimes. But the jail also accommodated some violent criminals. Two inmates were soon to be tried for murder, one for beating his girlfriend to death, the other for shooting a convenience-store employee who resisted being robbed. Another inmate was Dr. Ralston, a physician accused of sexually abusing boys.

Gene Alice listened attentively as we got the latch to open. She later told me that I was an exception to other boys she knew. "I had never had any boy talk to me as if I were his equal," she said. She also admitted she had been a bit surprised that I told her about the doctor. In those days, good boys were guarded about saying anything of a sexual nature to a girl. But I had spent much of my life in the presence of strong women. My mother and her outspoken sisters were not shy about what they said in front of me. They had no trouble fending for themselves. I never believed women were fragile vessels in need of a man's protection.

I knew the boys Dr. Ralston was accused of abusing. They were several years younger than me, all from leading families in the community. The company hospital was within a block or two of their homes. Ralston was a tall, urbane, handsome man with a quiet demeanor. Until he was charged as a child molester, Ralston was considered a great asset to the community. In the face of his accusers, he earnestly maintained his innocence, saying that he had merely befriended the boys. Perhaps it wasn't the best idea to invite them to his home and embrace them with "a fatherly hug," he conceded. That was his story.

I also told Gene Alice how strange it was for me to be a symbol of authority at the jail. Several times after I led a service, inmates asked to speak privately to "the preacher." It troubled me that, through the bars of the Hutchinson County jail, a teenager listened to grown men speaking in hushed tones and acted as their father confessor. In fact, it scared the hell out of me.

As our group was getting ready to leave that day, Ralston leaned against the bars and whispered, "You should marry that girl. I saw your eyes light up when you saw her smile. There is such a thing as love at first sight." I was taken aback. I'll admit I was smitten. But love? Marriage? Those words weren't in my vocabulary.

Before we left that day, the jailer invited the boys, but not Gene Alice, to take a tour of the facility. She leaned over to where I was tucking my notes inside my Bible. "That's the way it always is," she said. "The boys trot off for some interesting excursion, leaving me behind." Rather than leave her standing alone, I invited her to go with me to see a woman on the other side of the jail, in the women's section. Her name was Mary, and I told Gene Alice how I came to know her. One Sunday after the regular service, the jailer asked me if I would talk to Mary, a young, uneducated black woman. She desperately wanted to see "the pastor." Mary told me she was unjustly accused of child abuse and neglect. She had four children, and the oldest, a seven-year-old, was truant from school on a cold, snowy day. The school nurse was dispatched to determine why he was absent. When the nurse located the family's shack, she found Mary's four children huddled around a wood-burning stove that had very little wood left. Bedcovers were on the bare floor, and there was almost no furniture. The children were placed in emergency foster care. The police located Mary across town and arrested her. She was not able to tell her story because she was so frightened and worried about her children. When she reached out to me, she was totally distraught and barely intelligible. I finally calmed her and heard her side of the tragedy. She had no husband and was the sole provider for her children, who must be missing her terribly. Mary had tried to keep her family together by doing housework for families on the west side of town. Her employer for almost a year had recently moved to another town, leaving her to knock on doors and ask strangers if they needed a housekeeper. She had no telephone and no transportation. The nearest bus stop was almost a mile from her dilapidated house. That sub-freezing morning, she left her oldest son, the truant, in charge of the little ones, put on a thin sweater, and walked to the bus stop. She used her last bit of money for bus fare to go to the neighborhood where she had worked for over a year. She was knocking on doors when the police found her and hauled her off to jail.

"I'll never forget what she said next," I told Gene Alice. "'Pastor, I love my children and they love me. We need each other.'" I felt tears slipping down my cheeks as I remembered feeling helpless and horrible for Mary and her children. I took the hand of this beautiful girl I had just met and said, "That was her story, and I believe every word of it."

Standing outside her cell with Gene Alice, I wanted to weep again for Mary, when this fragile, emaciated woman reached out to take Gene Alice's hand, crying and telling her how grateful she was that "the pastor" at least took time to hear her story. For two West Texas teenagers, listening to Mary was probably our first raw encounter with the brutality of poverty and racism. Mary was the only black female inmate. Her cell was in an isolated corner, far down the hall from ten or twelve white women. I knew deep in my soul that meeting Mary had changed my life. I had only known Gene Alice for about one hour, but I suspected it had the same effect on her. At least, I hoped so.

Gene Alice was clear-eyed about her reason for being at the jail that day. On our walk to see Mary, she had confided that she was there only because she dated Donald Gene, the baritone in the quartet. I realized in that moment that, to her, I was a nice, harmless boy who just happened to be in charge of the jail service.

That fall I moved away from Hutchinson County to attend Baylor University, a Christian college in Waco, 440 miles from Borger. I had time to grow up a little before I saw Gene Alice again.

Chapter Four

In the fall of 1955, I was a junior at Baylor, when I saw Gene Alice again. Nearly three years had passed since that fateful day at the jail. I was heavily involved in student government and leading a project to help entering freshmen register for classes. We all knew registration was a confusing and haphazard ordeal, partly because Baylor was one of the few schools on the quarter system. A student had to understand that the normal class load was three courses that met Monday through Friday, leaving no day off between them. It was important not to get overloaded with more challenging courses or to take more than three. My job was to direct bewildered freshman to one of three student government helpers. That is when I saw a beautiful girl puzzling over a stack of papers. She wore a white blouse with a brown sweater draped over her shoulder, a flowing skirt, and brown loafers. No socks. A memory stirred me. Ah, those ankles. I walked over to her.

"Aren't you the organist I met at the Hutchinson Country jail a few years ago?" I asked her.

"Yes, I'm Gene Alice Wienbroer," she said, adding that she remembered that I had been the preacher. "Are you a ministerial student?"

"No way. After hearing the testimonials of those prisoners and talking to the woman we visited, I decided being a preacher was not for me. I'm pre-law. May I help you cut through this registration nightmare?"

She explained she was trying to sign up for three required courses but also wanted to take an exclusive English class in which the professor, Ernestine Fall, accepted only twenty students. Gene Alice was among them. But one of the registrars had told her she couldn't be in Dr. Fall's class because she had to take the three required courses. A tough fourth course would be too much.

"Follow me," I said. We walked to a table where we found Mrs. Markam, an assistant registrar and the wife of the dormitory director where I was a wing director. Wing directors and their assistants had coffee and cake every Monday night in the Markam apartment. As we approached, Mrs. Markam looked up.

"My goodness, Max, who is that beautiful girl? Is she your girlfriend?" I'm sure Gene Alice and I blushed.

"No, we met just once a few years ago at a church service. Now, would you believe, here she is at the same college! She has a problem I think you can help her solve."

Mrs. Markam spoke to Gene Alice and checked the catalog carefully. "I will sign the form to let you take your science required course starting next year," she said. "You don't want to have an overload when you're taking Dr. Fall's class. It will be a lot of work."

Problem solved. As we walked off, I blurted out, "Gene Alice, would you join me for a soda in the student union? We should get to know each other." My guess is she had no choice but to say yes after I had helped her. Our first conversation was over a frosted root beer. I already knew I wanted to ask her out, but I was afraid of being turned down. I remembered her telling me she was at the jail that day because she was in love with the quartet's baritone. I worked up my nerve and asked her point blank: "Are you still dating Donald Gene? You told me at the jail that day you thought he might be the one for you."

"He's a wonderful guy, but we have not dated for a while." She paused briefly, perhaps unsure of how much more to say and then plunged ahead. "My best friend Kathryn's father was pastor of the Church of the Nazarene. It was not my church, but throughout our high school years, I often attended services there. We would sing a duet together and I joined her church choir. Donald Gene was a devout member of that church, and he loved singing in the choir. That's how we met."

She became increasingly open and chatty about her relationship with Donald Gene, as if I were a girlfriend she was confiding in. "He was a super athlete, all-state in football and basketball. He and I hit it off. We dated throughout our sophomore and junior years. One evening, he made the fatal mistake of asking me to marry him."

Wait, they were in love, and he wanted to marry her. How could his proposal be a fatal mistake? She must have noticed the surprise I wore on my face. Gene Alice explained that they had spent a great deal of time together, including singing on the road, talking, and going to the movies. "But he did not know me," she finally said. "His world was athletics. My world was music and literature. He dreamed of being an All-American coach. He wanted to have a wife when he headed off with an athletic scholarship to help him with his coursework and to take care of the children."

And then her voice became a little louder and more emphatic: "Never, never did it cross my mind to marry a coach and be the custodian of the dishes and the diapers."

I made a mental note of "the custodian" phrase. Was she sending me a signal not to get any ideas? I almost chickened-out, but I managed to work up the nerve to ask her to be my date to a Foreign Film Club screening. We met at the student union and watched Federico Fellini's masterpiece, *La Strada*. It was Gene Alice's first foreign movie, but I could tell she was captivated, subtitles and all. She said she loved Anthony Quinn and was fascinated with Giulietta Masina, Fellini's actress-wife and muse. She vigorously joined in the group discussion. Afterward, she said, "How do I join? I don't want to miss a film."

I walked her back to her dormitory. It was a wonderful evening. I lay awake that night contemplating how I should ask her out again. I understood that dating and getting serious would have to be on her terms. The answer turned out to be easier than I had imagined.

We agreed that each week we'd see another film together, join in the group discussion, and then spend the rest of the evening dissecting it together. I don't recall how many times we were together during her first six months at Baylor, but our relationship must have advanced far enough for her to accept my invitation to celebrate her eighteenth birthday in February at The Chef, the most expensive restaurant in Waco. We dined on Dover sole. Made small talk. "Are you enjoying your classes? Who is your favorite professor?" After she gave her assessment of her first one-and-a-half quarters in college, I urged her to take a drama class that I had loved from Professor Paul Baker. "It will change your life," I told her. "It is the most important class I have ever taken."

Gene Alice weighed my words. She was a good listener and never seemed to be in a hurry to respond, even when she had a strong opinion. Sometimes, it was hard to tell what she was thinking. Her propensity was to analyze and make sure she had considered all sides. Finally, she said she wasn't sure she wanted to take the class, having never had a course in drama or theater. "My father started me taking piano lessons when I was barely five. My life revolved around piano, organ, and choral music and now courses in literature. Are you sure I would like it?"

"Absolutely! It's a drama class, but it is really about creativity. You would love it!"

Gene Alice and I were conscientious students. We spent many of our first dates discussing ideas raised in history, philosophy, and English classes. Several times Gene Alice asked me to help her prepare for an exam in Dr. Fall's class. It was a bit of a jab, I'm sure unintended, when she followed her request by saying, "That way you can vicariously take her class." I had previously confessed to her that I had unsuccessfully applied for admission. I agreed to help, and for both of us, it was a chance to be together in a non-romantic way.

She told me it was impossible to study in the tiny dormitory room she shared with three other women, so she found a large table on the fourth floor of the Carroll Library, which she considered her nightly study carrel. I started showing up with my bookbag, taking the seat across the table from her. I think she was glad to see me but mostly ignored me. We did not speak, just nodded. Every once in awhile, I would catch her glancing up to smile at me.

Gene Alice wasn't shy. She had many friends, knew what she wanted, and, as she had already shown me so many times, wasn't afraid to assert herself. Not in a mean, arrogant, or aggressive way. She had a quiet determination, a serene sense of confidence. She did not appear to be looking for ways to get to know me better, but I saw the way men looked at her, and I inserted myself into her life so as not to risk her losing interest in being my friend. One evening as the library closed, I worked up the courage to ask if I could walk her back to her dormitory. After that, it became a routine. Walking through the central quad one evening, she mentioned the drama class I had urged her to take. She wanted to hear more about it. "I may add it as an extra course next quarter," she said. We sat on a bench. I told her about the lectures, the suggested readings, and how students sit in swivel chairs surrounded by three stages for lectures and stimulating discussions led by Professor Baker and the theater staff.

"At my birthday dinner you were so passionate about the final exercise," she said. "Tell me more about it."

I told her I had had no idea what my final project was going to be because I was preoccupied with summer plans to go to southern Michigan and knock on doors, selling Bibles and books. I would be the crew leader for twenty-two male students I had recruited to join me for that second summer of working as door-to-door salesmen. It was a bit overwhelming! One evening, a friend from class asked what I was going to do for the final project. The deadline was looming, and I was still clueless.

"Remember that Professor Baker told us to be prepared for the creative idea to just pop into your mind? I guess that's what I am waiting for," I told my friend.

I told Gene Alice that on my way back to my dorm that night, I had to cross a bridge over Waco Creek. I looked down at the trickle of flowing spring water and thought this might be a starting point. Continuing through the open field adjacent to Kokernot Hall, I tried to force creative thoughts, the very thing we were told not to do. I decided to sit at one of the picnic tables and think through the project. One of Professor Baker's comments popped up: "Your creative project may start with a most unlikely abstract image." For some reason, I started to sketch the outline of my dormitory. It was a sterile, abstract outline: a roof and several floors of windows in straight geometrical lines. That was it. It was not inspiring.

When I got to my room that night, I told Gene Alice, I followed Professor Baker's suggestion to play with the abstract design. Trace and retrace the outline. Add color. Let the lines take on life. Keep those that take on personalities. I put the design on a large sheet of butcher paper and stretched it over a large table in my dorm's basement. I started walking along the lines. I began to feel a rhythm and even a bounce. At first, I imagined I was a boy carrying a trumpet in a marching band, practicing on a football field. It was dull, so I picked up the pace. I began to prance and dance. It was crazy. I was having fun. Some of the lines had sparks, some did not. I dropped the ones that had no bounce and tripled the size of the ones that made me want to jitterbug. This led to a crude musical score. The more powerful lines represented the brass. The fine thin ones, flutes or piccolos. It was no longer a thing. It had become a personality.

One morning, I took that abstract design to the football practice field to walk it out in the early morning dew. I could actually feel the rhythm. I now had an abstract painting of a lopsided triangle with a brightly colored hypotenuse and thin lines for the sides of the angle. And it was with that unlikely image in that unlikely setting that I envisioned a very different thing for my project. It was a brief story about a man who was the last person left in the world. He had created a beautiful flower garden, a piece of music, and a three-minute stage performance that he knew no one would ever see.

I told Gene Alice all of this. Then, I told her my project became a parable that I called "Dakota Brave." She wanted to hear it, and strangely, I could still recite it from memory.

"A Dakota brave stands in a meadow, wearing only a loincloth on his lean body, facing the setting sun at the back of the stage. His hands touch palm to palm above his head in a worshipful pose. The brave lowers his hands to follow the gradually setting sun as it moves closer to earth until they are prayerfully at his chest, close to his heart. Slowly, he bends his knees extending his arms out to the far reaches of left and right in perfect alignment with the horizon. In harmony with Mother Earth, he gradually sways, dipping and rising to occasionally glance up at the sky but carefully and softly picking up each foot.

"As one foot is safely on the soft grass he pauses almost as if in mid-air. His gaze focuses on a gorgeous butterfly gliding back and forth across the meadow. He dips and rises to perfectly mimic the harmony and grace of the butterfly. As if stalking a deer, he slows his pace and cautiously lowers his arms to reach down to pick up an imaginary butterfly net. His whole being knows not to step on a twig or make rapid moves that will scare away this beautiful spirit. After three gentle swooping movements, he succeeds and captures the butterfly. He pulls the net down and stoops to examine the vivid orange, brown, and yellow colors. After several moments of silent reflection, he gently shuffles the butterfly into a large imaginary bowl and carefully covers the opening with a piece of imaginary gauze.

"He looks down expectantly as he reverently lifts his captive above his eyes. His head moves from side to side as he examines the beautiful creature. His fingers flutter in pace with the rapidly moving wings of the frightened caged butterfly. The brave's face transforms from a pleasant smile to a sad countenance. He is troubled. The butterfly was celestial as it flapped its wings freely in the sky. The wings are now drooped to its side in its prison. He ponders, but then, hesitantly removes the gauze and gradually lifts his hand to let this beautiful spiritual being fly freely to the sky, following it with one outstretched hand and his own happy gaze. He smiles. The butterfly is free."

I was very surprised when I looked at Gene Alice's face. With tears in her eyes, she put her hand on my shoulder: "Max, please make a copy for me."

Several times on our walks through the quad she pulled out a well-worn copy of "Dakota Brave" and asked me to read it to her. I would do it but always asked, "Why does it mean so much to you?"

"It just does."

Only later did I understand why.

Chapter Five

I was falling hard for Gene Alice, but I wasn't sure what to do about it. Initially, I had been drawn to her beauty, but as I got to know her, I was just as enthralled by her intelligence, openness, and sensitivity. We were close friends, and she seemed comfortable with that. She did not act like she would appreciate being kissed, and I had to keep reminding myself to be patient. Don't touch. I needed a way to introduce romance into our relationship, to open up the subject. That's when I hit on something she already loved: poetry. I started to memorize love sonnets. One evening on our walk back to her dorm from the library, I told her I had memorized two sonnets. "May I say one of them to you?"

My heart pounded when she said, "I would like that." I had chosen Edmund Spenser's "Sonnet 75" and slowly recited the lines:

One day I wrote her name upon the strand,
But came the waves and washed it away;
Agayne I write it with a second hand,
But came the tide and made my pains his prey,
"Vain man," said she, "that dost in vain assay
A mortal thing so to immortalize,
For I myself shall like to this decay,

And eek my name be wiped out likewise."
"Not so (quod I), let baser things devise
To die in dust, but you shall live by fame:
My verse your virtues rare shall eternize,
And in the heavens write your glorious name.
Where, when as Death shall all the world subdue,
Our love shall live, and later life renew."

Gene Alice listened attentively and said she enjoyed it very much. That was all the encouragement I needed. On our walk the very next evening, I recited one of the most romantic poems in all of literature, Shakespeare's "Sonnet 116:"

Let me not to the marriage of true minds
Admit impediments. Love is not love
Which alters when it alteration finds,
Or bends with the remover to remove.
O, no, it is an ever-fixed mark
That looks on tempests and is never shaken;
It is the star to every wand'ring bark,
Whose worth's unknown, although his height be taken.
Love's not Time's fool, though rosy lips and cheeks
Within his bending sickle's compass come;
Love alters not with his brief hours and weeks,
But bears it out even to the edge of doom.
    If this be error and upon me proved,
    I never writ, nor no man ever loved.

I took her hand. Rather than try and say anything, I just gave her hand a little squeeze. I felt like our relationship was progressing beyond friendship, and I was learning how important it was to take an interest in her interests. Fortunately, we shared many of the same passions, like music. Although Gene Alice was an English major, she took every organ and piano lesson she could work into her day. She had a one-hour standing reservation to practice the organ in the Tidwell Bible Building three mornings a week. I started showing up each of those days and would sit at the back of the hall and simply listen. Afterward, we would walk together to her next class, holding hands.

Still, we kept it light and dated others. I preferred Gene Alice's company to anyone else's. We had so much fun together.

Once, we took a day trip to Dallas for me to attend a student government meeting. We left Waco early so that I could take her to an ice-skating rink. I helped her put on her skates. "I'm sure you don't remember, but the first time I saw your ankles was as I watched you pump the old field organ at the Hutchinson County Jail," I said. Spontaneously, she popped back. "I certainly don't remember that!" But she did not pull her foot away from my hands.

We picnicked in Cameron Park, which became our favorite spot. Often, on a rainy day, we would lie on a picnic table under an enclosure and just dream aloud, say poetry, or sing ditties. On a clear evening, we would lie on a picnic table and look at the stars.

One of my favorite memories is driving to the little town of West, about twenty miles north of Waco, and introducing her to kolaches from a tasty Czech bakery. She fell in love with kolaches. We often bought two dozen and devoured several on our drive back to Waco. We shared the rest with two married couples who were on tight budgets, living in cheap student housing. We were comfortable hanging around our young married friends.

The summer after her freshman year, she lived at home in Borger and worked as a clerk in the city tax office. I sold books and Bibles in Wood County, Ohio. We did not exchange a single letter. I began to wonder if I had imagined that we had been dating. True, we had never embraced or stolen a passionate kiss. It was not in our Southern Baptist DNA to have a deep romantic commitment. We were committed to getting an education. It was ingrained in us to not let anything interfere, especially a love affair, and certainly not sex. We knew that sex can really get you into trouble. We had seen some of our Southern Baptist friends have their plans and goals torpedoed by a dalliance that led to sex and babies.

Back at Baylor for my senior year and Gene Alice's sophomore year, we picked up where we had left off. That spring quarter, as my graduation was nearing, I realized that I didn't want our regular visits to end. One evening, Gene Alice and I were sitting on our favorite bench in the quad discussing summer plans. Within a week of graduation, I planned to head off, this time to Pennsylvania, for my fourth summer of selling books and Bibles. She had a summer job as a receptionist at one of the local carbon black plants. I looked into her hazel eyes, holding her hands and taking a long, deep breath before saying, "Gene Alice, I love you. Will you marry me? Let's spend the rest of our lives together."

I think she was shocked. After a long pause, she said the words that froze my insides. "Max, I do think we are falling in love. We might someday get married. I am just not there yet. I don't really think you are. You don't know what you want to do with your life."

She added that we both were dating other people, which was true, but I did not feel romantic toward anyone else. I assumed she also had no real romantic entanglements. But there was more. She went on to recount the many times that spring we had discussed whether I should take a military deferment, go to law school, go to Navy Officer Candidate School, or even take the six-month army program before deciding my next step. On top of that, I had told her repeatedly that I loved politics and might want to run for elected office.

Her future also was filled with possibilities. Recently, she had spoken with Dr. Fall about graduate programs at major universities. "I actually think I might be a university professor one day," she said. "I am only nineteen. I have a lot of thinking to do. When I was a little girl, I promised myself that I would get a college degree as a first step to fulfilling my dreams. We have so many unanswered questions. All I can say right now is, we just have to wait."

I could feel hot tears stinging my eyes. I did not want to cry, but my lip began to quiver. She put her fingers to my lips, "Shhh, you don't have to say anything. Let me explain. Do you remember that night when we were in Cameron Park lying on the picnic table looking at the stars? You started to sing a beautiful tune about love tapping you on the shoulder and catching a falling star to put in your pocket and save for a rainy day.

"I do think love is tapping us on the shoulder. I also think that our many unanswered questions may be our starless nights. Right now, I know that I will not be put in a pocket waiting for a rainy day."

She paused again but wasn't finished having her say. My mind was reeling, and I was in pain. It took all my strength to focus and hear her words. "Do you remember when I asked you to read the parable? You asked me why it meant so much to me. The only answer I could give then was, 'It just does.' Here is why I cry every time you read it aloud to me or I read it silently to myself. Most, if not all, of the females I looked up to as role models as I was growing up lived with dreams unfulfilled. Teachers who had one degree but not the graduate degree of their dreams. Housewives who dreamed of travel to New York City, San Francisco, or even Budapest, but who never got as far as Dallas or Oklahoma City. Church musicians who never got to hear a performance in any of the great cathedrals or concert halls. Even preachers' wives who never got to dance. The list is endless. In almost every instance the dream died by falling in love, getting married, and having children."

She continued her explanation. "I cried when you first read the parable to me. I saw myself as the butterfly. I love flying free and dreaming. I do not want to be cooped up in a bowl or placed in a pocket. I could not explain then, and it's hard now because I do think we are falling in love, and I am very happy when I'm with you. But, Max, I am still the butterfly. I just have to fulfill my dreams. I don't know where I will fly, but I have to be free to try."

That night as we walked back to her dormitory, we did not hold hands. Her desire to wait was more than a roadblock. To me, it was a rejection. It was almost as if she said, "No way. I'm not marrying you. I'm not really in love with you."

Had she misread me? Was I just like Donald Gene? Did she think all I wanted was a wife to help me through law school, to sacrifice her career for mine? Did she think I was just an indecisive, confused, immature boy, scared not to know what lay ahead and out of fear had blurted out, "I love you," and then stumbled into a marriage proposal? Did she simply fear that if I went away to law school we would not see each other again? Did she think she might fall for some other guy? Was this the end?

Chapter Six

I lay awake for hours that night scolding myself, "What in the world came over you? Why would a twenty-two-year-old Baylor student propose marriage when he had promised himself not to fall in love until he completed his education? You have three-and-a-half years of law school ahead of you. Are you crazy?"

I considered again that I was not the only guy attracted by Gene Alice's beauty and brains. She liked to tease me. One evening when we were having one of those frosted root beers in the student union, she told me about a man from her summer job in Borger. She was the switchboard operator at one of the local carbon black plants, which use a byproduct of incomplete oil combustion as a pigment for rubber. The switchboard was across the aisle from several administrative officers' desks. She sat in a tiny enclosure just large enough for her to turn her chair in a circle. She entered and exited by a swinging wooden gate. After her first few days on the job, the junior executive, whose desk was nearest hers across the aisle, asked her to leave the gate open so that he could see her lovely legs and ankles. She took the comment as a joke and did not feel threatened.

In those days, "sexual harassment" wasn't even a term. Anyone who knows people of a certain vintage or who has seen *Mad Men* is aware that many men harassed women co-workers and that women rarely objected because they had no recourse. They'd be shown the door if they complained. I do not condone this behavior and never did. But the 1950s were very different than life today. It was not uncommon for friendships to develop in spite of treatment that should never be tolerated. Gene Alice and the young executive were no exception. They worked together and were good friends throughout the summer. They even saw a few movies together. To her, his behavior was merely teasing. To me, it was a warning: He's a threat. Don't let her get away.

And then there was Ralph. He posed a far more serious threat to me. Gene Alice accompanied a young men's and women's quartet as they performed at churches throughout Texas, Arkansas, and Louisiana. Ralph was a ministerial student and the tenor in the young men's quartet. He went on the same trips as Gene Alice. Two of the women in the quartet were from my high school. Like Gene Alice, they were three years younger than I. They knew Gene Alice and I had been on a few dates, and they had seen how Ralph behaved around her. It seemed to me they enjoyed spilling the beans. "We think Ralph is in love with Gene Alice," they told me. "He told Hugh, the baritone, he was going to ask her to marry him! You better not let her get away!"

One time, as Gene Alice and I were dancing, she told me her version of the Ralph story and admitted he had proposed to her. But she told me she responded with these words: "I just can't do that, Ralph. I do love you, but I could never be a minister's wife. My grandmother and my mother long ago warned me not to marry a preacher. Granny married a preacher, and throughout her life had to hide her snuff box. Tavia, my mother, lived in fear he would discover how much she loved an off-color joke. I have my own reason to say 'no.' I love to dance. You must find another girl you love who will be happy married to a preacher. That's just not me."

Like many events in the lives of those of us who grew up in a conservative, evangelical church, I tried to find a religious or, at least, a biblical explanation for my impulsive proposal. I was trying to explain my opposing feelings of wanting to marry this amazing young woman and knowing that it was absolutely impossible for me to get married while I was seriously thinking about law school. Seeking to understand my conflicting desires, I returned to my Southern Baptist roots and the story of "The Prodigal Son." Is it possible that I was a third son that the well-known Bible story had missed altogether? I was not the younger brother who left home for the glamour of a faraway land, nor was I the older brother who was comfortable with the security and safety of home. Was I a third son who wanted both security and glamour? When I blurted out, "Will you marry me?" was I grasping for a way to ultimately have it all in one beautiful, smart girl?

"I have to take some time to sort this out," I told myself.

"Let's not see each other for a while and see what happens," I told her.

A blackout followed.

Chapter Seven

Gene Alice and I vanished from each other's lives. I headed off to Lancaster County, Pennsylvania, to peddle Bibles and books. I brooded a lot. The Southern Baptist in me urged me to pray about our relationship. That was tough. I wasn't sure God cared that much about a spat between two young Texans struggling to find themselves, but I did try. On the Fourth of July 1957, I took a holiday from knocking on doors and stopped off at a rural Catholic Church. It was close by, and I wasn't going to be picky about denominations when asking God to lend me an ear. I slipped into the small sanctuary, sat to contemplate my future with Gene Alice, and prayed. I tried to imagine life without her and couldn't. Whether the Lord spoke to me or whether I simply decided, I came away with this message: "At least send her a card."

I did not know where she was or what she was doing, so I mailed a postcard to her Borger address. I admit that a lot of thought and prayer went into selecting the card and the few words I could put on it. It was not at all romantic. I attempted to summarize what I had been doing that summer. As I recall, it was a brief travelogue about going to New York City, Atlantic City, and Amish country. I signed off with a stiff "auf Wiedersehen."

Coward! I put a return address on the card and waited every day for a reply. None came. By the time I returned to Texas, I was deep into preparing for law school. I had been accepted by the University of Texas at Austin, 500 miles from my West Texas home. I put Gene Alice out of my head but not my heart.

Chapter Eight

Everything I had ever heard about the pressure-cooker atmosphere that is the first year of law school was true. I was terrified when I learned that one-third of my grade would be determined by three exams over three yearlong subjects: contracts, property, and torts. First-year students could get a snapshot of how well they were performing by taking midyear exams that did not count toward the final grade. I spent many long nights and wee morning hours preparing for my first exams. I feared those exams might tell me I was in the wrong place. Then what? I also was stressed for another reason: I was scared to distraction thinking that I might not ever see Gene Alice again.

I had done quite well working my last summer as a door-to-door salesman and crew leader with twelve new salesmen scattered around southern Pennsylvania. I ended the summer with a nice bank account. Impulsively, after studying all night the first week in December, I decided to trade the 1953 six-cylinder Ford my mother had bought me when I retired John Crupper's Lincoln Continental for an upgrade: a 1957 pale-green Chevrolet Bel Air. I loved driving it but soon realized it was no consolation prize. Gene Alice wasn't around to admire it or ride in it, and try as I might, I could not forget her.

To cope, I again sought the help of a higher power. On a Sunday, days before Christmas, I worshiped at the University Baptist Church in Austin. In the sermon that morning, the preacher made a passing reference to T. S. Eliot. That was all the encouragement I needed to knock on Gene Alice's door in Borger two days later.

Often during my last quarter at Baylor, Gene Alice and I would sit on one of our favorite outdoor benches and discuss poetry from a course I had taken on T. S. Eliot. Together, we fell in love with *The Love Song of J. Alfred Prufrock, The Waste Land, Four Quartets,* and *The Hollow Men.* The instructor, Ms. Carroll, was passionate for her eight students to not just read poetry, but to become part of the poem. She wanted us to know that these were more than words on paper. They were alive, real, personal. Ms. Carroll taught us to have our fists in the air when we read them, just as she had done once with her students in a crowded basilica at the Vatican in Rome. Mussolini had just given a rousing harangue from the pope's balcony. The passions of the crowd were at a high pitch. Toward the end of Mussolini's blustery speech, the crowd surrounding her was shouting with raised fists in the air. To make her point, Ms. Carroll was startled to find her fist raised and pumping in the Italian air. She had become part of Mussolini's fascist poetry.

For the long drive from Austin to Borger in my new Bel Air, I prayed and rehearsed what I would say to Gene Alice. Six months had passed since I sent that postcard with a return address. Six months since she had not replied. Was she telling me it was all over, and was I now playing the fool? Would she even welcome a visit? I was terrified. I had ordered and paid an exorbitant amount to have a shoo-fly pie express-shipped to me from the Dutch Haven bakery in Rook, Pennsylvania. I thought it offered a light-hearted excuse to knock on her door.

When I arrived, Gene Alice and her mother, Tavia, were having a cup of coffee and discussing what Gene Alice was going to do after graduation from Baylor. Her mother answered the door, coffee cup in hand. Gene Alice said later she glanced over to see me standing there grinning like Alice in Wonderland's Cheshire Cat. I handed Tavia a box with the shoo-fly pie and offered a greeting I had rehearsed, "Merry Christmas from Amish country!"

Tavia invited me to join them for coffee and pie. I was flabbergasted. Gene Alice was still in her pajamas. But there we were, sitting at her family's kitchen table as I told stories from my first semester in law school and from my Bible-selling summer in Lancaster County. Not only had I come with a pie, I came armed with the church bulletin from the University Baptist Church two days earlier.

"The sermon, *Journey of the Outsiders,* was so powerful," I said. "May I tell you about it?"

Tavia, the daughter of a Baptist minister, immediately said, "By all means."

In those days, University Baptist Church might have been the most progressive Baptist church in the nation. In 1950, under the leadership of Dr. Blake Smith, it started welcoming blacks and whites to worship together, four years before the Supreme Court reversed its position on race by declaring that "separate but equal" was no longer the law of the land. Smith started his sermon the Sunday before Christmas by telling us that God revealed the coming of his Son to the shepherds and the wise men, not to the Jewish church leaders, the Pharisees and the Sadducees. He said the wise men weren't even believers. Rather they were intellectuals, astronomers, and scientists who came to Bethlehem on a scientific search, following an unusually luminous star in the North. The shepherds and wise men were "the outsiders" in Smith's sermon. They were not the only ones. Smith then related a recent experience when he was the speaker at an event focused on religion and life at the University of Colorado at Boulder. A group of students had invited him to join them at a pub where they planned to continue dissecting one of his sermons. Smith said he had asked the students to each relate something that had drawn them closer to God. One of the young women said that reading T. S. Eliot's play, *The Cocktail Party*, had brought her much closer to God. That was Smith's brief reference to a poet Gene Alice and I both loved. As I finished summarizing the sermon, I considered the odds that I would be in church that day to hear T. S. Eliot mentioned. It reminded me of my chance meeting with Gene Alice at the Hutchinson County Jail. I felt like I was getting the message to go and see her.

Weeks before my bungled marriage proposal, Gene Alice and I spent a full evening discussing the meaning and significance of a few lines from Eliot's *Four Quartets* in which he addresses his soul, calling it to heel, requiring that it wait without hope or desire. Gene Alice and I foresaw the rough road ahead. How could we be together with me in Austin and her in Waco? How often would we see each other? We concluded that Eliot was speaking to us in those lines, to have faith in what is to come. Wait. Have patience. We said a little prayer that there would be light in the darkness and dancing in the stillness. I knew instinctively that neither of us was prepared to say, "I love you," and, certainly not, "Let's get married." Why had I forgotten that?

Chapter Nine

In my history of dating, the invitation I issued to Gene Alice during our time at home for the holidays certainly was not my most glamorous. "Would you be my date New Year's Eve to babysit my niece and nephew? Sheila is three. Jimmy is one. My sister, Billie, and her husband, Richard, are going out to a New Year's Eve party. I think you will enjoy the kids."

I was surprised and elated when she said, "I would like that." Neither of us had a better offer, and babysitting offered a comfortable New Year's Eve: no raucous party, no alcohol, no dancing. Our Southern Baptist upbringing frowned on those evils. Even so, we both loved to dance.

The early part of the evening was pure, simple fun: games, piggyback rides, running, laughing. We tucked Sheila and Jimmy into bed and then sat side by side to read *The Cocktail Party*. Gene Alice found the only hardback copy in the Hutchinson County Public Library, probably the only one in the Texas Panhandle. She handed me the copy and said, "Let's read it aloud to each other." I'm not sure if that evening brought us closer to God, but it was the beginning of bringing us closer to each other.

At the stroke of twelve, we hugged and kissed. It was not a passionate kiss, just a Southern Baptist peck on the lips.

After Billie and Richard returned at two in the morning New Year's Day 1958, I drove Gene Alice home. As I was leaving, she took charge of our relationship. "Max, let's just start over. We haven't seen each other for several months. Right now, we are good friends. We may even be in love. Let's keep seeing each other whenever possible but also date other people. Let's see where the future takes us."

I offered to return the book to the Hutchinson County Public Library. Because the library was an old comfort zone where I had spent hours researching and preparing for high school debates, I sat down to read a couple of newspaper accounts of the Broadway production of *The Cocktail Party*. It had received the 1950 <u>Tony Award</u> for Best Play. I jotted down a page of notes from the critics to share with Gene Alice. "*The Cocktail Party* simply plays its characters in a crucible of choice and diagnoses their indecision as a malaise … with the major symbol of the consequence of choice being The Cocktail Party itself in a somewhat tiresome modern world. ... It is the burden of the human race to face tough choices, and live with the consequences. Each and every person is offered a choice and must make one … though it is not very illuminating to be told that 'the right choice is one you cannot but make.'"

I was a bit overwhelmed with how the play had spoken to me. What do I do next? Where will I go? With whom will I go? Will it be with Gene Alice? Do I go alone? I prayed that I would make "the right choice."

I did not agree with Eliot that it would be the only choice I could make. It would be *my* choice. It was not predestined.

When I returned to Austin, I immediately went to the University of Texas campus bookstore where I found two copies of Eliot's *Complete Poems and Plays, 1909-1950*. Gene Alice and I had agreed to discuss an Eliot poem or play whenever we were together. I wanted to be prepared.

Chapter Ten

After our New Year's Eve date with T. S. Eliot, I wrote a few letters to Gene Alice from school in Austin. I'm not sure she wrote back. I think she was letting me incubate. My few letters were basically chitchat, almost as if we are walking and talking or sitting on a favorite bench in the quad at Baylor. I mentioned books I was reading, classes I was taking, plans for my last summer selling books. In one, I made an oblique hint that I might have realized the mistake I made to propose marriage, writing, "It's amazing how time, people, and everything changes. Dean Green (my torts professor) once said that only in chaos was there eternal life. Things die, decay and from this, people or new life come forth to try to improve on the past. Maybe he had something."

Other than a few dates to grab a Coke with women in the dormitory where I waited tables, I did not really date anyone. The second semester of my first year in law school was so critical because it was the one where you must bear down to prepare for those big three final exams. Two women friends in a singing quartet told me Gene Alice was dating "a guy from Baylor law school." He was on the same campus as she, and several of my Baylor friends were in the same fraternity with "the guy." I knew that even at Baylor, these fraternities regularly hosted cocktail parties. My hope was they were just as tiresome to Gene Alice as those in Eliot's play.

My almost daily letters to Gene Alice reminded me of how desperately I missed our talks about books, movies, plays, poems, ideas, doubts. As if we were sitting side by side, I wrote to her, saying, "Remind me to tell you about the Beat Generation, *The Catcher in the Rye,* Alec Guinness, Frank Lloyd Wright, *The Family Reunion,* and the like." I concluded with a long quotation from Holden Caulfield in *The Catcher in the Rye* and closed with, "But I'm crazy. I swear to God I am."

Chapter Eleven

N ear the end of my first year of law school, a postcard arrived. "Let's stay in touch," it said. "Here is my summer mailing address." I learned that Gene Alice and two of her best friends at Baylor, Barbie and McGoo, were going to summer school at the University of New Mexico in Albuquerque, taking courses to ensure they would graduate a semester early, in December. I later received a note from Gene Alice with photos showing me how much fun they were having hiking in the mountains, putting down a pallet, and studying in the warm sun. It said, "My fantastic Shakespeare professor encouraged us to find our own private nook and read the poems and plays aloud. I love doing this at my private spot on the mountain."

To let her know that I was not just selling Bibles, I wrote that I was reading *Rebecca* and *The Uses of the Past.* "It takes a pretty sharp person to take advantage of the education nature offers and also the one dished out by the men and women of the ivory tower. So, start quoting your Shakespeare by the light of the glowing sun and wiggle the toes on your bare feet." That same letter captured the ambiguity of our love life.

"What's next?" I asked. "You will be finishing at BU by mid-semester, won't you? What are your plans after that? Europe?

Asia? New York and the UN? There is still the University of the Philippines, you know. … Don't study too hard and let me know about all of your wild excursions."

The truth is, I really didn't relish hearing about how much fun she was having. Without me. I didn't want to ask about the law student she was dating because, frankly, I didn't want to know. Every mention of her dating or enjoying someone else's company felt like a knife carving out a piece of my heart. Obviously, I needed to make a move, if it wasn't already too late.

Chapter Twelve

I had no master plan for reconnecting with Gene Alice. My recollection is vague of our first meeting after a long drought. The best I can recall, I just showed up in Waco, called her, and asked if she would join me for the homecoming football game. I'm sure our time together was much like our first visit at Baylor's student union. Getting acquainted, or, in this case, getting reacquainted. I invited her to be my date to my law fraternity's big annual dinner dance in Austin in November 1958. To my relief, she accepted.

Then, a minor miracle occurred.

Twenty-three-year-old pianist Van Cliburn, who had startled the world by unanimously winning the first International Tchaikovsky Competition in Moscow on April 13, 1958, had accepted an invitation to perform at Gregory Gym at the University of Texas the same weekend as the fraternity party. It was one of his first American performances after being christened the world's greatest pianist. Cliburn, who had been welcomed back to the United States with a ticker tape parade, had become an instant star. The Elvis Presley Fan Club in Chicago had changed its name to the Van Cliburn Fan Club.

I luckily got two of the last tickets. I asked Gene Alice to stay over another day so we could go together. It was one of the most memorable days of my life. We sat in the bleachers in Gregory Gym; Gene Alice leaned over to whisper in my ear, "It is almost like being on top of Kilimanjaro." She was captivated by the tall, young Kilgore, Texas, resident just as much, and maybe even more so, as the Communist judges. That night we dined on chopped steaks at the historic Night Hawk restaurant, which set me back $1.50 per plate, complete with a baked potato and salad. She humored me by ordering a slice of coconut cream pie, my favorite, with two forks.

Afterward, we took a pallet to Zilker Park and lay down to look at the stars, just as we had done so many times at Cameron Park in Waco. We relived the day, still gushing about having seen Cliburn in concert. We shared a deep, abiding love of music, whether it was classical, country or swing. Although Gene Alice was a musician, in addition to being a fine singer, I also loved to sing and watch bands, orchestras, and virtuosos perform. That night we crossed the bridge that I had long considered "the bridge too far." We exchanged passionate kisses, far different from that New Year's Eve peck on the lips.

As we cooled down, I lost my head and blurted out before I realized what I was saying, "Let's get married." I was stunned. Never had I thought of violating her admonition that, "We just have to wait." I knew from our conversations at the homecoming game she had applied for a prestigious Ford Foundation Scholarship at the University of Wisconsin in Madison to study an experimental way to teach literature. In my hazy memory, I think her response was almost identical to her rejection of my first proposal that night on the quad. "Max, I may love you, but we have to wait. I am only twenty years old. I am committed to getting a graduate degree, maybe even a PhD. You have a year-and-a-half left of law school.

We both know the military hangs over your head. You don't know where or if you will practice law. I can't even think about marriage until the direction of our lives is clearer."

We walked to the car without holding hands and spoke few words as I drove to her overnight accommodation. She had a room for the weekend with Nancy Ann Golightly, Tavia's friend since their freshman year at Wayland Baptist College in Plainview, Texas. I saw Gene Alice to the door of the Golightly home. There was no goodnight kiss. I was hurting. Quite possibly, she was upset with me. As I turned away, I wasn't sure whether to give up or beat myself up. All I could say was, "I've got to think about this some more."

I had a lot of time to think about it.

Chapter Thirteen

Several of our mutual friends from high school and Baylor kept me up to date on Gene Alice's plans. I think all of them hoped that we would eventually get together, but I also realized what mattered most is what she thought. I had come to understand that, to Gene Alice, the idea of marriage represented the end of freedom, not the start of something new and wonderful. She wasn't about to be captured in a jar like a butterfly that had only just begun to sail on the wind.

From the moment I stepped away from the Golightly house after hearing that second no, I felt like I was wandering in the wilderness. At first, I was in such a funk that I repeatedly scolded myself: "Don't you dare write her a single letter! Don't call her! Don't make any attempt to see her again! Don't you dare go by her house or knock on her door when you are home for Christmas."

I had my pride, but now it was in tatters. I retreated to dark thoughts and told myself lies to salve my ego. I had heard plenty of sexist comments in the locker-room, and though I never joined in, they rang in my ears. "Don't get involved with a smart girl. She will want to wear the trousers," they'd say. Or, "When I marry, it will be a gorgeous blond who knows I am boss." And, "Marry for beauty not brains." I always believed these were the foolish ramblings of insecure men. Now I questioned everything I had believed. As I said, I was lost.

I suspected Gene Alice wanted to be another Ernestine Fall, with a doctorate from a prestigious university, married to the classroom. Clearly, she did not want to be married to me. I had thought love was enough for us, but I could see that it wasn't. Besides, I didn't know whether she had ever loved me. I had been such a fool to think we'd be married.

Two weeks after that second no, I spent half a day polishing silver, crystal glassware, and a champagne ice bucket. I put white linen on my tables, carefully smoothing out the wrinkles. Each table had eight place settings. I was ready to spend my evening serving my "girlfriends" and their dates at the annual Christmas dinner party at the women's dormitory where I had waited tables since I started law school. It was the big event of the year. A big band was hired. Girls were encouraged to wear formal evening gowns. Because some did not have dates, the rules were relaxed. Waiters were allowed to dance with the young women they served during the day.

Karl, a fellow waiter and one of my closest friends, was moonstruck over Betty, a stunning woman. They had been out on several dates. He was convinced that she was the one he should marry. He wanted to be sure Betty felt the same way. He asked me to invite her to dance and find out. She was the talk of the waiters; I couldn't let down a friend. My Southern Baptist upbringing did not prepare me to dance with a beguiling beauty with a much different background from her two years at a New England girls' school. Shakespeare must have had Betty in mind when he wrote about the dilemma of a confused, frustrated, testosterone-charged young man:

"Love's not Time's fool, though rosy lips and cheeks
Within his bending sickle's compass come…"

Betty danced so close. I knew I was in trouble. I had not felt this way since I had been with Gene Alice. In fact, I had been completely miserable as I focused on my law review assignments and Gene Alice's dating life. Suddenly, I wondered if Betty might be "the one" for me. Or maybe it was someone I had yet to meet. I replayed a discussion Gene Alice and I had had several times. Should I join the Navy and take three years to sort things out? Should I look for a job at a law firm? What about politics? My indecisiveness was stalking me. I wanted Gene Alice's advice, but I had no idea where she was. If she had graduated in December, she could have gone anywhere to pursue her teaching career.

I broke a promise to myself and wrote her a letter in January 1959. I was so frustrated and uncertain I had to reach out for help, but I did not know where to send the letter. I mailed it to her mother with the request that she forward it. My rambling letter left little doubt about how mixed up I was.

"Sometimes I don't even understand my own erratic self," I wrote. "Why, for example, have I let you get away from Baylor without even knowing where you are? For this reason, I am sending this to Borger in hopes that it will reach you wherever you are."

Gene Alice wrote back with her thoughts and ended with, "Well the Gay Philosopher is signing off now. I'll try not to be surprised when I receive your next communication in Timbuktu, via Borger, some three-and-a-half months hence. Gene Alice."

Then nothing for some time. I was at a loss on what to do next. I tried in vain to forget about her. When several waiters invited me to a raucous party in a rambling house they rented together, I was happy to put my worries aside. Betty was there with Karl. I did not have a date. I just sat, watching others dance. Betty told Karl she was going to ask me for a dance.

Did we dance. It was whirling, writhing, slow dancing, close like that first time at the dormitory event and nothing like the proper way Gene Alice and I danced. I was spooked. After my third dance with Betty, at her invitation, Karl pulled me aside. "Max, it's obvious Betty and I are not going to make it. Right now, she is flirting with you. You should go for it, for all its worth." Karl was disappointed, but maybe he had grown tired of Betty's flirtations. I welcomed the distraction.

A spring fling became a boil. All conversation and discussion of ideas, books, or movies gave way to seizing every moment for a passionate embrace. Law school studies were put on hold. Thoughts of Gene Alice were put on hold. Common sense was put on hold. A summer of long, daily phone calls culminated in an unexpected re- union when Betty showed up in Austin from her home in Oklahoma City. She had come to talk about getting married. We had a long, torturous conversation about life and values, goals and aspirations, all of the things Gene Alice and I took for granted. But those were not Betty's plans. We argued over what each of us expected out of life. There was no "God plan" to pray and let things work themselves out. Betty laid out her plan from start to finish. She wanted *things*. A big law firm. A quick rise to partnership status. Lots of money. Country club membership. Prestige in the city. Great parties. Her ambitions resembled the "tiresome modern world" Gene Alice and I had discussed derisively many times. We had agreed that it was not our dream.

That was my last date with Betty.

Chapter Fourteen

Gene Alice, armed with Dr. Fall's unequivocal endorsement, won the Ford Foundation fellowship at Wisconsin. But because she was so young and had never taught school, the foundation required that she first complete at least one year of teaching. Baylor placed her as a sophomore English teacher in Texas City, a busy port on Galveston Bay. Home to manufacturing and petrochemical plants, it was known for the 1947 explosion of a ship laden with ammonium nitrate that killed 576 people. The city rebuilt, and by the time Gene Alice arrived, the high school was in a gleaming new building and paid one of the best starting salaries in the state. It was glamorous, as public schools go, and English teachers taught only four classes. Texas City was much like her hometown of Borger in population, industry, and smell. The people, particularly the teachers, were friendly and accommodating. Gene Alice told her longtime friend Barbie that she had only one complaint against her new home: Out of her first five weeks there, only eight days were sunny. She did not live too meagerly but saved as much as possible for her new life as a student in Madison.

In my mind, Gene Alice and I were back to being friends. I decided to write to her in that context, and she wrote back, evidently in the same vein. She told me some things about her life I did not want to hear:

"I spend almost every evening and most weekends preparing for classes the next day or week. I have no social life. My closest friend is another English teacher married to an officer at Ellington Air Force Base just thirty minutes away. Her husband's best friend is Rick, a fellow officer and pilot, a recent engineering graduate from Purdue University with a three-year commitment to the Air Force. One evening her husband said, 'Rick has no social life and your friend Gene Alice has no social life. We should introduce them.'

"The introduction worked. Rick and I now see each other whenever he has a leave. He loves to fly and is considering a career in the Air Force. We dine and dance at the Officers' Club on base. For the first time in my life, I spend evenings in what in Borger would be called a bar or a tavern. I still maintain my Southern Baptist upbringing. I don't drink alcohol. I always have a Coke."

I was strangled by jealousy. I imagined them, a striking couple, turning heads everywhere they went. I suspected Gene Alice was fully enjoying her freedom and had forgotten all about our passionate kisses in Zilker Park the evening of my ill-fated proposal. I did not tell Gene Alice how I felt about her dates with Rick. Then came her next letter.

"Last night Rick called to see if he could stop by my apartment. He brought take-out Chinese food and a six-pack of beer for him and a carton of Coca-Cola for me. We were having a great time.

"He was excited to tell me about the round-the-world flights he had been on over the last two weeks. It was a one-sided conversation. He was so tight that he would never let me interrupt to tell him about the poetry I had introduced to my class over the same two-week period. A poem by T. S. Eliot, a sonnet by Shakespeare, and a love poem by Elizabeth Barrett Browning. He was exhausted from talking so compulsively. He assumed he would spend the night with me. I ushered him out the door with, 'Oh, no. You are not spending the night. You have to go. That will be our last date!'

"I knew that I would not marry a coach or a minister. I certainly was not going to stay involved with a career military man whose main conversation was to relive his exploits and showed no interest in my life other than to go to bed with me.

"To top off this miserable experience would you believe that the very next night, after I kicked Rick out of my apartment, Texas City had one of its frequent rainstorms. The rain was so heavy that it drove two-inch-long cockroaches under the entry door of my musty apartment. I had only seen small West Texas cockroaches. That was the final straw.

"The head of the Baylor placement office was disappointed when I called to tell him I had to leave roach-infested Texas City. An unexpected position as an intern to an executive secretary at J. C. Penney had just crossed his desk. I immediately accepted the position with the assurance that I would fly to New York City as soon as school was out."

Gene Alice was going alone to the Big Apple for a summer job and could not have been happier. She would return to the public schools when they reopened in the fall and finish out her year-long teaching commitment. For now, freedom and adventure beckoned, and Gene Alice answered.

"I am so proud of myself," she wrote later. "I made all of the arrangements … I found a sixth-floor apartment at Evangeline House in Greenwich Village, a residence for women between the ages of eighteen and fifty who are in the city for professional work, education, or a trainee program like mine at J. C. Penney. I can easily and quickly find my way around the city. Evangeline House is near every subway line and some crosstown buses. In just ten minutes, I can stroll through the Meatpacking District. The East Village is a great spot to have fun with new friends. The West Village has some of the best restaurants, great venues to spot celebrities. I love to shop in SoHo. It is a dream come true."

The young woman who grew up on the West Texas plains did not seem at all intimidated to explore all that the nation's largest city had to offer. Surely, the experience would change her, and I wondered if she would be seduced by the big city and decide to stay. I didn't have to wonder for long. Gene Alice sent another letter near summer's end.

"I have had two sobering experiences that let me know that New York City is great for a summer, but not for me long term," she wrote. "The first occurred when my roommate's newly acquired stereo set was stolen from our apartment. On the sixth floor of our apartment building, a thief swung from one wing of the building into our apartment to enter through an open window to take all of her stereo equipment out the front door. The very next week the Big New York City blackout hit. My roommate was away with family, so I was all alone. No electricity. No air-conditioning. No lights. I sat in the dark on the sofa with the windows wide open listening to the *On the Waterfront*-like calls from across the rooftops. 'Hey, Enricá. Hey, Enricá.' I did not have a gun, but I did have a butcher knife. I knew I could defend myself.

"The second sobering experience was when my boss at J. C. Penney started asking me out for dates after work. We had meals together at great restaurants and often went to local bars and pubs. Alan usually had one or two martinis and I had a Coke. I knew that many of these outings were paid for with his expense account because I handled the paperwork.

"The conversation was not quite as one-sided as Rick's, but most of it revolved around J. C. Penney and how well things were going in his division. My day of secretarial duties was not very stimulating, and Alan had no interest in poetry and literature. One evening as we were taking a taxi for Alan to drop me off at my apartment his two martinis got the best of him. He asked if he could come in and spend the night. That was it. I immediately replied, 'I have to go. My roommate is expecting me.' That was our last date. In his defense, I do think he thought we might have fallen in love.

"Not long after the blackout and the spurned invitation to spend the night, I asked Mama if there might be a teaching position in Borger. I need to complete the requirement to have at least one year of teaching in a public school. There is, so I will move back to Borger."

Well into the next academic year, Genie sent another letter. "I moved back to my mother's home, sleep in the same bed that I did as a young girl, eat at the same kitchen table, and continue to learn to be a teacher. I teach sophomore English in the same local high school from which I graduated and in the same room where I sat as a sophomore. But, I'm glad this teaching requirement is underway and that I left New York City.

"After I returned to Texas, Alan called several times to offer me the position as his executive secretary. He gave me a one-year's subscription to *The New York Times*. Shallow, but nice.

"At the end of the school year, I will head off to Madison, Wisconsin." And she did. She had saved enough money to buy a brand new 1960 VW Beetle. Her butcher knife was tucked under the car seat during the day and beside her bed each night in the motel.

Chapter Fifteen

My third year of law school was starting, and I realized that an anchor in my life would soon disappear. For nineteen Septembers, I had been a student and never had to worry about what would come next. Now I was worried, and I had plenty of company. All of the guys who were not veterans had the same anxieties. After graduating with a law degree, we could be drafted into the army for a two-year term, maybe get a commission in the Judge Advocate General's Corps and serve three years, or take one more year of law school for some specialization to get beyond the age to be drafted. Another option was to sign up for six months of active army duty at a post somewhere in the United States followed by seven years in an army reserve unit. Not pleasant thoughts for a budding lawyer. I huddled with several law review friends to hear about their plans and get advice. They all had offers from big-city law firms. I was a year younger so my offers were contingent because I would be subject to the draft for one more year and might not be able to join the firm. What was the best way to juggle law, military, and in several instances, romance? None of the guys was married, but all had serious relationships. Except me.

Three of us planned a summer 1960 trip to Europe. We would depart right after taking the bar exam to backpack through

Europe. We had brochures from travel agencies and copies of *Europe on 5 Dollars a Day.* Not one of us would admit that we were just postponing important life decisions.

Midway through the bar review cram course, my future travel companions came to tell me they were backing out of our European adventure. One was getting married; the other was accepting an offer from a big firm and signing up for the six-month military program.

Gene Alice and I had once shared the dream of going to Europe. One evening on the quad when I was expounding on such a backpacking trip, Gene Alice said, "Max, you should do that. You'll have fun and it is a great time to think and work things out."

I decided to go alone. I needed time to figure out how to unwind the tangled mess I had created. Hiking through the Scandinavian countries, I made an attempt to return to the common ground of books that Gene Alice and I so often shared. I read and reread my paperback copy of Ayn Rand's *Atlas Shrugged.* I knew that Gene Alice and I would agree and disagree with so much of what I was reading. I so missed those exchanges. I pulled out my well-worn copy of the letter she wrote in response to the distress signal I had sent her in Texas City. I repeatedly read the following paragraph.

"As I read back over the preceding, it's unsatisfactory. Unsatisfactory in the way that all letters are unsatisfactory: they don't talk back to you. In this sense humans & human conversation really have it over letters & letter-writing." We exchanged a few other letters, but I didn't carry any of the others with me. I didn't want to think about all of the men who tried to sleep with her. I missed her counsel and well-thought-out arguments.

I hurriedly hitchhiked to Oslo to change my airline ticket. I returned three weeks earlier than planned. My first stop was to see Tavia, who became my Southern Baptist priest. Tavia knew more about Gene Alice and me than either of us had imagined. "It is not for me to say that you and Gene Alice are destined for each other, but for several years I have watched the two of you struggle with that question. It is something the two of you must work out. Call her." Tavia gave me her daughter's phone number.

Chapter Sixteen

Before I dared to call Gene Alice in Madison, I reread my tattered copy of her letter to a distraught law student, which I nicknamed the "gay philosopher letter."

"Now, about you, Mr. Sherman. First, I suppose I should scold your neglect & then sudden appearance in the mail. But not being of a scolding nature myself and knowing that you do and will continue to do what you very well please, and since I have been too occupied myself to lose any sleep over your ordered existence, or lack of, in law school — well, I really don't think a scolding is necessary."

I knew that whatever lay ahead we had to meet and chart a course that we'd take either together or separately. I called. She said, "I will meet you in Chicago."

—

Chapter Seventeen

As Gene Alice made what I am sure was a lonely drive from Madison to Chicago in her dark-blue Beetle, she had a lot of time to think. On my TWA flight, I had time to think, too, but I also was praying. I relived our treasured times together and shed tears as I castigated myself over my two ill-fated marriage proposals. I did love her. I was beginning to understand her deep desire to live fully as Gene Alice, not a butterfly in a jar, especially a jar held by a man. From the moment I first met her on that walk through the halls of the Hutchinson County jail, I knew that she was a girl who would fulfill her dreams, with or without some guy. She was confident that whatever her destination, it would be the right destination, and she would decide how to get there. Her fate was not tied to anyone, and if anything, she had only grown more self-assured and confident. I fretted over what we would say to each other. How could I convince her we belonged together? I felt like the betrayer approaching the betrayed.

As I stepped off the plane into the terminal, a stunningly beautiful woman wearing a sleek gray-blue dress was watching at the gate. Our eyes met. Her face looked troubled, but she smiled. I flashed the best smile I could muster and waved. When I caught up to Gene Alice, I knew it would not be a good idea to spend time rehashing the last tortured months. "Let's pick up where we left off, two friends talking ideas, movies, and books," I said.

We took in two museums, the Field Museum for Gene Alice, The Museum of Science and Industry for me. She suggested that we go back to our first date at Baylor and see a foreign film. While waiting at the airport, she had read a review from the *Chicago Tribune* of the newly released Russian movie about a soldier returning home, *Ballad of a Soldier*. I am now convinced that it was a symbolic choice because I was wounded and hoping it was possible to go home again.

That evening we drove to Madison. After years of almost reading each other's mind, we must have had a lot to say. But the unanswered question still hung over our heads. Did we have a future together? She was living in a rented room in a row house designed by Frank Lloyd Wright in his early years. Ms. Ihlenfeld, her landlady, agreed that I could sleep on the sofa. There we were, sleeping in the same house, one on the sofa, the other in a tiny bedroom only ten or twelve feet away. I should explain that for me and Gene Alice, there was non-sex sex. Sex says go all the way. Non-sex sex says go all the way emotionally, but not all the way physically. In today's world that may sound strange, but every single situation I was in with Gene Alice was non-sex sex. It is a Southern Baptist interpretation of unbounded love, a love beyond the physical world. I loved Gene Alice's essence, the core of who she was: wise, loyal, caring. If I had only cared about beauty, I might have succumbed to Betty. But values mattered, and Gene Alice's and mine were in harmony.

After two wonderful days together in and around the campus of the University of Wisconsin, I knew that healing would take time. The big question between us would remain just that. Unanswered.

I returned to Texas, and in November, I entered the army. I had chosen the six-month active duty option, with an eight-year commitment to the army reserve. I boarded a bus full of young men heading to Fort Leonard Wood, in the Missouri Ozarks. Many letters flew back and forth between Madison and Fort Leonard Wood. One day, I read the most important sentence of my life. "I now know that I love you," Gene Alice wrote toward the end of one of her letters. Was the butterfly ready to break out of the chrysalis?

Gene Alice and I were experts at dancing with ideas, with words, with movies, with music. We had many of those dances in our relationship. And we could cut a rug. We had never been ready to do the tango, that raw, sensuous, mating dance from Argentina. Was Gene Alice's statement an invitation to swoop in and tango with her?

Chapter Eighteen

Gene Alice drove her Beetle from Madison to Fort Leonard Wood. I was in my final assignment, learning to operate heavy equipment in an engineering unit. She spent her first night in the guest barracks, only to be awakened by cannon blasts that heralded the flag-raising ceremony. It was just outside her window, announcing the time, six o'clock in the morning.

Because I had a five-day pass, I invited her to the northern Arkansas home of Will and Adocia Davenport, my blood grandfather and step-grandmother, the only grandmother I ever knew. It was a snowy winter weekend in February 1961 when we set out in the Beetle. It did not have a heater other than the heat coming from the motor, controlled by a valve between the two front seats. It kept us warm, but as soon as we got out of the car in front of my grandparents' home in the Ozark hills, the ice, snow, and temperature took over. We were bone-cold.

No one was home, although I had carefully let them know our arrival time. There was a note on the door. "We are at the church. Come join us." I knew they meant the Gum Springs Baptist Church, which I had attended regularly during my growing-up summer visits with them. Later, as I would come and go to Nashville, Tennessee, during the five summers I sold Bibles and other books, I always stopped over for a few days with Will and Adocia. One of my favorite memories was the time Will invited me to preach at church one Sunday when the itinerate preacher failed to show up. I produced a sermon from my notes in that same perfect-attendance Bible I had taken to the Hutchinson County Jail. It was also the sermon that dispelled any expectation of my relatives that I was called to the ministry. After the worship service, the whole congregation would gather at my grandparents' home for a potluck meal. Will was the patriarch of the community. He was a big man and usually sat in a straight-back chair in the side yard. He asked me to sit on the grass beside him for some advice. "Max, that was a nice talk," he said of my sermon. "I hope you will come back and preach for us sometime."

That memory washed over me as we cranked up the VW and drove down the rutted gravel road to the church. It was packed inside and heated only by the warm bodies of the congregants and one big Ben Franklin wood burning stove, sitting near an upright piano.

In a letter, I had told my grandparents that Gene Alice was the granddaughter of a Baptist minister, a fantastic musician, and a wonderful piano player who had accompanied the choir at the Calvary Baptist Church. As soon as we arrived and shook the snow from our coats, the regular accompanist jumped up to invite Gene Alice to play while the congregation sang. It appeared to be a done deal, and all of the churchgoers were prepped. The "girl" Max was in love with was treated as a member of the most important family in the area, the Gum Springs church family.

The music came from *The Songs of Stamps-Baxter Choral Collection*, which Gene Alice had never seen. She played for thirty to forty minutes of singing. When someone requested "Oh, Those

Beautiful Hands," she looked at me for help. I just shrugged my shoulders. She had accompanied choirs and choral groups all of her life but never a hill country singing like this. She instinctively adjusted to the swing and bounce of a congregation that lived and breathed "a good singing." After the service, every single member of the Gum Springs family gathered round to give Gene Alice a hug and thank her for helping to make a cold night so warm.

We went back up the hill to my grandparents' home, also heated by a single big Ben Franklin stove. On the way, she told me that she had never had such a good time. "It was like electricity. So, so much fun."

My grandparents had reserved what had always been my room for "Max's girlfriend." I was moved to the tiny bedroom just off the bathroom. Gene Alice's bedroom was outside the kitchen door, just off the back porch, right across from the cistern, which was the sole source of water. It was an uninsulated room with one large double bed. There was no heater, and it was freezing cold. Gene Alice later confided that she almost froze to death. She slept in her traveling clothes, put all of the clothes in her suitcase over the covers, and piled on every available material in the room.

After Gene Alice turned in, I sat with Will and Adocia around the stove. Adocia pulled her chair next to mine and reached over to pat me on the leg. She was a true woman of the hills. As far as I knew, she never traveled more than fifty miles from Gum Springs. She was one of the biggest influences on my young life. Although I was barely out of the womb when my mother and I moved to Texas, Eva had friends and relatives who would deliver me back to Fulton County, Arkansas, for summers with my grandparents. Will farmed and had only a wagon, two horses, and one mule. He lived without a car or electricity and toiled from sunup to sundown, milking the cows and cultivating the soil with a plow the mule pulled.

Adocia was my buddy. When I visited as a small child, delivered by my mother's relatives or friends, Adocia bathed me in a galvanized tub. As I got older, she instructed me to bathe in the cold stream on their property. Quietly, in her soft hill country voice, she coached me on cleanliness. "Always wear clean clothes," she would say. A fond memory is her tucking me into bed and pulling the blanket up around my neck and giving me a hug. I always felt deeply loved by her.

As I got older, she spoiled me by letting me be her constant companion, working beside her in the garden, churning butter, and picking blackberries, cherries, and peaches. The most fun of all was helping her cook. She taught me how to make chicken and dumplings. I loved rolling the dough. A favorite treat was to cut off little strips, glaze them with butter, sprinkle cinnamon and sugar on them, and pop them in the wood-burning stove to brown.

She also taught me to overcome my fear of the dark, dank cellar. She would carefully negotiate the rough, concrete steps to descend into the cobweb-laced dungeon to get a bowl of sauerkraut, kept in a heavy, wooden crock. When she came back into the natural light, she always patted me on the head to reassure me. "See, Max, I'm OK. There is no one down there. Do you want to help me sometime?" Eventually, I worked up the courage to slowly go into the dusty cavern. Sure enough, there was no one down there. Even with her frail, small frame she had lugged the heavy crock over to a spot close to the last step so that a bit of outside light made it easy for me to find. I lifted the lid, scooped up a bowl of sauerkraut, and hurried back to the kitchen. After several such journeys, I started taking a coal oil lantern down to explore the other treasures of the cellar: jars of canned sausage, pickles, peaches, cherries, and even a few hidden bottles of whiskey.

As a Bible- and book-selling college student, I had often seized on any opportunity to visit Will and Adocia. She always gave me that same hug just before I drove away. She probably was a bit under five-feet tall, and her shoulders were stooped from all the heavy lifting. As a young man, I had to bend down for that hug.

In the warm glow of the wood-burning stove the day I brought Gene Alice with me, Adocia said, "Max, I watched you and Gene Alice down at the church as you glanced back and forth to send signals. As Will and I walked home I told him that I thought God ordained that you and Gene Alice were meant for each other." She patted me on the leg, "Pray about it as you sleep tonight."

The next morning, Gene Alice and I were up with the dawn, having a cup of coffee at the kitchen table. I told her that she had not only stolen my grandparents' hearts, but the hearts of the entire Gum Springs community. "They did not ask you to 'Come back and preach for us sometime!' You preached their kind of sermon as you pounded the piano. It was a loud Gum Springs Baptist Church 'amen' as they lined up to hug you."

As we made the 350-mile drive back to Fort Leonard Wood I heeded Adocia's words. I was still praying.

ACT II

Chapter Nineteen

In the most unromantic setting anyone can imagine, a Howard Johnson's restaurant in West Plains, Missouri, I reached across the table, avoiding plates of pancakes and syrup, to take Gene Alice's hand. For the third time, but this time premeditated, prayer-inspired, and Adocia-encouraged, I said, "Gene Alice, I love you and I think you love me. Will you marry me?"

This time, she smiled and did not say no. She promised to give my proposal serious consideration. I wanted an enthusiastic "Yes!" Still, I felt hopeful as I stepped out of Gene Alice's car. When I did, she roared off for Madison, having nearly 500 miles to cover and two classes the next morning. I was suddenly left alone with my thoughts and had a lot to sort out.

Our visit with my grandparents in Arkansas reminded me of our Van Cliburn concert date. I had the overwhelming feeling that we had breached a barrier and were closer than we had ever been. That gave me the courage I needed to propose a third time. I would be lying if I said I wasn't nervous as I recalled the high from the concert and the low that immediately followed. Clearly, our relationship had reached a crossroads, a point beyond friendship, beyond return. I knew my own heart, but I did not fully know Gene Alice's. I thought she loved me and knew we could never go back to being "just friends." If she rejected me this time, it would be over, and I would lose her forever.

That was always the thought I could not bear.

I had come to realize I had no desire to spend the years that stretched ahead without hearing her voice say my name or talking late into the night about a movie or play we had just seen. I could not imagine what it would be like to never again hold her in my arms, kiss her soft lips, or stroke her hair. A part of her lived inside of me, and I believed I would lose an essential part of myself if I lost Gene Alice. I wanted her to be the partner I confided in about everything, the partner I woke up beside every morning, the partner who helped raise any children I would father. She was my soul mate, and I knew I would be beyond lucky to marry her.

From a journey of knowing with certainty to a journey of being stalked by questions with no apparent answers, I searched my soul for the path forward. The possibility that mutual love wasn't enough for a happily ever after occurred to me, but I was fortunate to have just enough hope to keep going. Almost daily, love letters from Gene Alice appeared in my mailbox at Fort Leonard Wood. She received the same written sentiments from me at her apartment in Madison.

Gene Alice's first letter was fairly mundane. "I'm home. And I must've picked up some of your tricks because the little bug and I made record time: off at 6:30, home at 5:00 — 10 1/2 hours. How about that? A nice day, many memories, so a pleasant trip." She did sign it, "I love you."

From that point on, she and I signed every letter with "love" or "I love you very much." Still, there were warning signs that marriage may not be in store for us.

One came soon after our trip to Arkansas. We rendezvoused Easter weekend in St. Louis with my old high school friends, Harry and Helen. Harry was a brilliant Rice University grad on his way to becoming a distinguished pediatric neurosurgeon. Helen was a lovely person, a topnotch tennis player and a University of Texas honors business graduate. Harry was in a residency program at St. Louis University; Helen was a secretary at a lumber yard. As Gene Alice and I drove back to Fort Leonard Wood, she was uncharacteristically quiet. I finally asked her what she was thinking.

"I feel so sorry for Helen," she began. "She is just as smart as Harry, but she lives her life in his shadow. As you know, my mother was recently named Teacher of the Year in Texas. That would never have happened had she not divorced my father. She would still be living in Bernard's shadow! Still under his thumb."

Her message to me was clear: That kind of marriage is not for me.

I was happy to see her handwriting on an envelope in my mailbox a few days later. "Your letters mean a lot to me, Max, even those short notes when there's nothing more important than to note that you love me," she wrote. "It seems that since the few days together at Easter, I am trusting you more and more. I don't know whether you understand the significance of this to me but it feels very good and I'm glad."

Translation: "Max, be patient. I'm working on it."

Chapter Twenty

In our almost daily letters over those next few weeks, we continued our careful dance: details about what we had done that day (KP and latrine duty for me, Chaucer and Hemingway for her), movies seen, books read, and questions raised about religious faith or lack thereof. In a Sunday letter, I described a military chapel service I had just attended and added this PS: "As I addressed this letter to Miss Gene Alice Wienbroer, I can't help but think of my grandfather's remark: 'It doesn't look much better than it sounds.' The trouble they had with your name!" Perhaps my not-so-veiled message was: Gene Alice Sherman surely would look and sound better. I knew she was still testing the water. She invited me to Madison after I mustered out of the army, before returning to Texas.

In my last three weeks of active duty, I took a physical, had an exit interview, and eventually got an ETS, Expiration Term of Service. Monday morning, nine days before my last day of active duty, I wrote to Gene Alice. "The telephone system at Ft. L.W. was on the blink yesterday. I should start processing Wednesday (May 3, 1961) so I'll wait until I've seen some of the other fellows leaving on my date before I try to call again. By that time, I'll know whether I am coming by car or bus. One way or the other, I'll be there."

My Wisconsin buddy left three days before I was released, so I had to make a bus reservation. There was only one route, and it required a long stopover in Racine. Gene Alice insisted that she meet me there so that we could make the 105-mile trip back to Madison together. As she put it in her letter, "It would be silly for you to sit out a long layover alone when we could be together."

Much like the time she met my flight in Chicago, I spied her first, awaiting my arrival. She was sitting in the coffee shop across the street from the bus terminal, drinking from a cup but able to see the bus pull in. I felt fluttery inside as I gazed at her profile. She turned toward me, and I was looking at a seductive but wholesome twentieth century Mona Lisa with her side-swept bangs, short hair, and smooth skin. I found the way her hair fell over her left eye and the swirl of hair that formed a cradle with a curl over her forehead very sexy. She must have felt my eyes on her or noticed that the bus had pulled up. Within seconds, she was in my arms. We hugged and kissed and loaded my small suitcase into the trunk of her car. She asked me to drive.

Heading down the highway, I asked, "Did you receive my second letter from last Monday night?"

She had. "You were reliving the drama exercise about the brave and butterfly," she began. "As I recall, you said that the design and the short story suggested freedom and that the butterfly was the stage medium. I totally agree. But what does that mean for us now? What have we learned in the years since you first asked me to marry you? You go first."

"Well, most importantly I love the butterfly and don't want to lose her. I now realize that if we might have a life together, it will be on equal terms. The butterfly and the Dakota brave will jointly say, 'Let's get married.' Yes, they'll say it together, at the very same moment. May sound crazy, but that is what I have learned. What about you?"

"I have learned a lot, but to sum it all up, I love you, and I want to be someone. I'm afraid that won't happen if we get married. I love to teach. Texas City was brutal trying to corral football players almost my age. But several of them told me how much they enjoyed reading the stories, and that made it all worthwhile. Borger was sobering. Teaching in the shadow of my own high school, I was fortunate my fellow teachers embraced me and continued to help me. Having the starting quarterback on the football team move from an F to an A-plus is one of my finest memories. Teaching with Mary Spoletz in Madison's graduate program was one of the most important times of my life. It taught me that a woman could be creative and very important in the lives of kids with so much underappreciated potential. And Mary reminded me of Dr. Fall. These are two extremely competent women, and they are my role models. Yes, they are married to the classroom, but their work completes them."

She concluded by saying, "I also learned that I would not be somebody as the wife of a military officer or a big-shot corporate executive. I already knew that I could not live under the thumb of a Baptist minister like my grandfather."

I tried to focus on my driving and not the pain swelling in my chest. I had been listening intently to Gene Alice and wanted to understand her. Did she truly believe I wanted her to live in my shadow, to give up her dreams for mine? Did it have to be this stark, either-or proposition? As silence engulfed us, I recalled a letter I had once received from her dear friend, Nancy. Nancy's mother and Tavia were best friends from their high school and college years. In response to my asking her what she remembered about Tavia's and Bernard's divorce, Nancy wrote:

"One time my mother said to Tavia, 'If only you had never met Bernard and had to suffer so much.' Tavia became very angry. She told Mother, 'Never, never, never say that to me again. I loved Bernard. I have two beautiful and wonderful children that I would not have had otherwise. I would still be married if he could have controlled his anger and greed.'"

In the middle of the twentieth century, I understood that women did not enjoy the same rights as men. I knew it was wrong and understood a reckoning was overdue. But I also wanted understanding. I hoped Gene Alice knew I would never be an overbearing or dictatorial husband. I wanted to have children with her, and I believed, in her heart of hearts, she wanted them with me. How could she have that if she were married to her work?

I did all I could to make clear that I was on her side and had no intention of being the kind of husband her mother and my mother had married. I told her that I considered marriage to be an equal partnership and had thought of what a marriage between us would look like. We would each support the other in ways that would allow both of us to fulfill our dreams. We would equally share the household responsibilities, with one of us handling the finances six months of the year and the other handling them the next six months. We would have one automobile until we could afford a second. We would take turns being chauffeur to the other. We would have children. I wanted five; Gene Alice wanted two. She would get her graduate degree, and I would seize every opportunity to be a successful lawyer. Our home would be a happy place for raising a family and entertaining our friends. And we would not borrow money except to buy a house or another car.

The terms of our partnership, which I christened the Wisconsin Plan, were left on the table. And, as so often happened in our relationship, Gene Alice charted the path ahead. She changed the subject.

"We will have two-and-a-half days together. Let's just be together," she said. "You will take the train back to Amarillo, and Monday morning, you will be a junior lawyer at the firm. I will finish my Chaucer paper and then the one on Hemingway's *Old Man and the Sea*. Let's write letters and share our lives as we have done for years. Then, let's see where we are."

Chapter Twenty-one

After two days together in Madison, we were back in the VW Saturday morning headed to Chicago where I would board the train to Amarillo. In letters that crossed in the night, we both confessed to sleeping long hours to catch up on our almost forty-eight hours of constant conversation. Gene Alice said she slept "round the clock" and then worked five hours in the library. I fell asleep the moment I took my seat on the train and did not wake up until I saw the instantly recognizable dusty landscape of the Texas Panhandle. I took a seat behind the desk in my tiny office at the law firm in Amarillo at 7:30 the next morning. My mind was on other matters besides researching case law for legal briefs.

Daily missives flew between Texas and Wisconsin. I described the details about doing the grunt work of a lawyer in training. She told me about her research and preparation for papers and exams on famous literary writers.

That Friday morning, May 19, the phone rang in my end-of-the-hall office cubby hole. When I picked up, the familiar voice on the other end said, "Let's get married." That was it. We had decided.

Chapter Twenty-two

It wasn't a dream. Gene Alice had accepted my proposal. She confirmed it in a letter that same night saying, "I just wrote Mother that for sure I'm coming home. I told her that if you hadn't said it was okay with you, I think I would have shot you on the spot — I don't know what with — verbally, I guess. Actually, the way I feel now, there was never any decision to make because nothing, just nothing, could keep me from coming home to you. No choice at all. Whoever talked about free will?"

I was ecstatic, but once again, I recalled Nancy's letter. Gene Alice lived her first seven years in the Bernard-Tavia household. She witnessed marital love and an overbearing husband. After she said, "Let's get married," did she have a deep, maybe unrealized confidence that if we have beautiful and wonderful children and it doesn't work out, we could get divorced? The thought did not thrill me, and I tried to put it out of my head. We did not discuss it, but I knew it could happen if I got out of line.

I immersed myself in work and waited for Gene Alice to come back to Borger. She and her brother, Carl, arrived in the Beetle the first week of June. A letter from R. A. Selby, assistant superintendent of schools in Amarillo, awaited her. Through the network of teachers and the recommendations from her year of teaching in

Borger, Selby was offering an appointment to teach English at Palo Duro High, a relatively new school in Amarillo. The kicker was in the letter: "All teachers must arrive at their school on August 18."

The University of Wisconsin's graduate program would have to wait — for now. Two lovers and their families were now on a crash course for a late-July wedding, less than eight weeks away. We had to pick a date, choose a church, get invitations out, decide on attendants, and, most importantly, find a place to live. The VW, Aunt Irene's old Mercury, and various family members and friends burned up the fifty-mile stretch of highway between Borger and Amarillo, assisting with preparations.

Gene Alice desperately missed playing music, especially the organ. By mail and telephone, she made arrangements to take a weekly organ lesson from Doneta Weatherly, the organist at First Methodist Church, a beautiful, historical red brick edifice in the heart of downtown Borger. There was no doubt our wedding would take place there. It met Gene Alice's exquisite aesthetic taste, and no wedding for her would be right without an organ. First Methodist had the best one in town.

Our resources for securing a home were meager. Gene Alice was to receive $380 a month for nine months of teaching, and I made $400 a month as a new lawyer. In our Wisconsin Plan "partnership" negotiation, we added an amendment: We committed to saving fifty dollars a month, starting with our first month of marriage. I made a list of four duplexes, as one of my senior partners urged me, saying, "Rent and then buy a duplex to give you an additional source of income," and added one upstairs apartment. I thought the apartment was too small and cumbersome, going up and down stairs, carrying groceries, laundry, and books. When we were able to scout out my list, I was quickly overruled. No duplex, too drab.

The upstairs apartment is perfect. Great address, Cheyenne Terrace tucked away in Old Amarillo. Serpentine streets. A room with a view, even though it is over the roof of the entrance to the house, and it makes a balcony. A private staircase, even if in the center of the main house. Two-story red brick. And a park close by.

"You will have to insist that Ms. Hess (the owner) put in a window air-conditioner and fix the broken light over the stairway," Gene Alice told me.

Taste prevailed. It was ten dollars a month more expensive than the ground floor duplexes I favored. I was getting a foretaste of our partnership.

Chapter Twenty-three

When it finally came, I realized I had been longing for this day for over eight years, since that chance meeting at the county jail. All because Gene Alice had a crush on another boy. We were married a few miles from the jail, on July 29, 1961. Following the tradition of the church we grew up in, I did not dress until I arrived at the church. I put on my suit and painted the brown soles of my shoes black so as not to detract from the ceremony when we used the kneelers at the altar, our backs to the congregation. Gene Alice emerged from the dressing room wearing a white silk brocade dress with an ankle-length skirt and a veil covering her short, curled hair. She was so gorgeous it took my breath away. I almost had to pinch myself to realize this was no dream. Standing beside Gene Alice was her best friend, Barbie. These two tall, beautiful women would have turned heads in any setting, and here they were, surrounded by a group of guys at a church altar: The Reverend Jessie Allison, me, my best man Tom Ed, and Gene Alice's brother Carl, who escorted her down the aisle. Our mothers, Eva and Tavia, were in the front pews; neither of us had a living father. An assortment of friends and relatives looked on as we dedicated ourselves to each other "as long as we both shall live."

We followed the ceremony with an evening reception at the church's fellowship hall, featuring punch and cake. I should state that the punch most certainly was not spiked, nor was there any dancing. But Gene Alice had her own silent protest against the rigidity of the church that had dominated much of her life. The place cards at the tables contained a quote from Lewis Carroll's "The Mock Turtle's Song:"

"Will you, won't you, will you, won't you, will you join the dance?"

After the reception, Gene Alice and I hurried off to the changing rooms to dress more appropriately for the hourlong drive that lay ahead. Gene Alice came out in a stunningly stylish suit of silk shantung, with a cropped, bronze-colored skirt, finished off with arm-length, cream-colored gloves. I changed from a tux into a suit and tie. We hugged our family and friends and jumped into our 1960 VW Beetle to drive to our new upstairs home in Amarillo. We cuddled side by side in the car, nudging our warm bodies as close together as possible. With a full moon that lit the road like daylight, we turned off the headlights during the twelve-mile stretch between the small town of Panhandle and the westbound road to Amarillo, gliding safely along in a state of sheer bliss.

We spent our wedding night in the apartment and rose the next morning to set out on our road-trip honeymoon. We spent the first few days at a remote cabin in the mountains of Northern New Mexico. We hiked, cooked, ate watermelon, played cards. I unsuccessfully tried to teach Gene Alice to play chess. After an hour of explaining the board and the importance of the king and queen and then, the bishops and rooks, she lovingly, but forcefully told me, "This is not what you do on a honeymoon. It takes too much time." She was the boss. No more chess.

To maintain my half of the Partnership, I secretly made reservations at the Broadmoor, a five-star luxury hotel in Colorado Springs. After several days exploring the mountains of New Mexico and really getting to know each other, we packed up the car and drove north for four more glorious days. The Broadmoor campus offered several opportunities for us to enjoy our new life together: an ice skating rink in a separate building, where I helped Gene Alice put on skates as I did on that day trip long ago in Dallas; a giant theater where we had a fabulous evening of entertainment from Harry Belafonte; and a world-class zoo up the mountain from the hotel.

The Cheyenne Mountain Zoo is the highest zoo in America, carved out of the mountain at an elevation of more than 6,700 feet. Two odd encounters there stand out that I later recognized as omens for our marriage. In the first one, we stood with a crowd of about twenty a few feet in front of the glass-walled cage for a fully grown, 400-pound gorilla, the world's largest primate. The gorilla loved to entertain. He would swing on a bar from one side of the cage to the other, put his nose against the glass, cut his eyes from one side to the other, almost seeming to smile as he surveyed the crowd. His entertainer instincts must have given him the thrill of picking one person in the audience to be his foil. He chose me that day.

The gorilla glided back and forth to the oohs and aahs of a gathering crowd. We all watched as he stopped on the far side of the cage, the farthest he could get from Gene Alice and me, bowed his head down to a trough and filled his mouth with water. With huge bulging cheeks he surveyed the crowd and then sent a stream of water across the cage that would have hit me in the face had it not been for the glass. I instinctively leapt back. The animal started swinging again. I changed my position to be more obscure. He found me quickly, stared into my eyes, and repeated the water-spewing episode. Then, he bowed. The audience applauded. We had just been entertained by one of God's most powerful creatures.

As we strolled over to a concession stand to have a frosted root beer in the warm sunlight, we laughed as Gene Alice said, "I could see that water streaming down your face like giant crocodile tears. You would have been a mess." Holding hands, we ambled past other exhibits to feed giraffes sticking their noses over the rail, throw corn kernels to peacocks, and share our frosted root beer with a baby elephant after the attendant told us, "He will love it."

We soon found ourselves at the Island of the Lions exhibit. We watched the largest alpha lion pace back and forth on the other side of a moat surrounded by spiked fencing and water. He was huge. He also entertained, but in a more menacing sinister way. He surveyed the much larger crowd as he paced. Gene Alice and I watched from the far-right side of the enclosure. The lion stopped, appeared to look me straight in the eye, and then, baring his glistening teeth, let out a ferocious growl. Almost in unison, the crowd drew back a couple of steps. The lion hunched, staring at me for what seemed an eternity, then started to pace again in front of the hushed crowd. I moved to the far-left side of the lion. The crowd was aware that something was going on as they watched me move and then turned to the lion as it continued its slow methodical pace. He continued pacing at the center of the island, almost as if he were on center stage in a theater, about to deliver a soliloquy. The lion made two or three threatening paces the full length of the island. Then, he leaned forward in what appeared to be a lunging motion, looked straight at me, and gave a second ferocious roar. The audience gasped. Had there not been the moat and fencing, the scene might have ended with the lion mauling me to bits. I was safe, despite having been singled-out, once again. The powerful lion was trapped, a captive on an island. It was as if he and the giant gorilla were reading from the same script. But what was the message? I would have to wait.

Chapter Twenty-four

As a wedding gift, the law firm increased my salary by fifty dollars, which meant that I supported the Partnership seventy dollars more per month than Gene Alice did, or 8 percent more overall. At a time when men pretty much ran everything and were expected to be the primary breadwinners, the raise made me feel a little more comfortable. But that was short-lived. The pianist who played during services at two funeral homes was pregnant and had to give up both gigs. She recommended Gene Alice take her place. Three or four services a month paid twenty-five dollars each. With three services, Gene Alice made five dollars more a month than I was being paid. With four services, thirty dollars more. Once again, I was the junior partner. When I pointed this out over a glass of wine one evening, Gene Alice laughed and said, "Let's keep it that way." And that is just what we did. I could not help her teach a class and certainly could not play the piano. She was a masterful English teacher and offered to be my editor for legal briefs, speeches, and any other papers I had to write. In return, I rubbed her neck as she sat at our kitchen table late into the night grading papers.

After one year in the upstairs apartment, a friend from church asked us to come over to see a little house on nearby Milam Street. The friend's mother had lived there and had just passed away. The family wanted Gene Alice and me to own it because they thought we'd be good stewards of the property. They would sell it to us for $9,500, the same price their mother had paid for it several years earlier. At 800 square feet, it had two bedrooms, one bath, wood floors, a tiny dining room, a living room, an extremely small kitchen, and an attached one-car garage. With a thirty-year mortgage at a very low interest rate, we took $500 from the savings and loan where we faithfully deposited our fifty dollars each month and had our down payment. The Partnership moved into its new headquarters. We could now entertain as we promised we would do under the Wisconsin Plan.

Chapter Twenty-five

As a young lawyer, I found the work to be tedious, monotonous, and exhausting. I spent long hours in the library researching legal issues for other members of the firm, reading advance sheets, and taking notes on recent court decisions. Oftentimes, I would bring advance sheets and the state and national bar journals home to read. It was not very exciting for Gene Alice, either. Unlike a book or a movie, there was nothing very interesting to discuss.

One Saturday night, while perusing the *American Bar Association Journal*, I saw a notice about something called the Ross Essay Competition on the subject of the year, "World Peace Through Law." I looked over at Gene Alice, whom I had begun calling "Genie" from time to time. "As I recall, you and I both took Professor Paul Goren's graduate class on the United Nations," I said. "You might find this interesting. You made an A-plus and I made an A-minus! You were his favorite student." She laughed as I handed her the journal.

After mulling it over for several minutes, she said, "I am not a lawyer so I can't submit an essay, but you can. If you will do a draft, I will edit it. It would be something legal that we can do together." I knew I could not do the research on law firm time, but I agreed that it could be a fun project for us. I made a list of books I would have to read past midnight while I worked on the essay, and Gene Alice found most of them in the Amarillo Public Library. We were off on a legal journey together. I handed her my first draft. After several edits and redos, we submitted our magnum opus. Gene Alice declared it "pretty good." The essay did not win, but it did get an honorable mention with an invitation to attend a session at the association's annual convention in Montreal, Canada. The senior partners at my law firm were so pleased that they said the company would cover all expenses for the two of us to go.

Gene Alice and I boarded the Santa Fe sleeper train in Amarillo, stopped off in Chicago, dined at The Bakery, which we had discovered when we met to determine if we might have a life together, changed trains, and arrived in Montreal a few days early. We were able to get a room at The Laurentian, the main convention hotel, with the assurance that we would relinquish the room as the delegates arrived. Our reserved hotel was in a suburb twenty miles from the convention site. We had three days for a second honeymoon. We spent one day driving through the Laurentian Mountains and stopped at a fabric shop for Gene Alice to select an elegant bolt of wool from which she designed a smart-looking suit. I marveled at her innate ability to choose colors and styles that were just right for her. She was always exquisitely dressed and appropriate for the occasion. Her wardrobe wasn't flashy or meant to be attention-getting. She put quality above show and wanted to honor every single thing she did by looking her best and being her best.

We spent two days and one night in Quebec City. Just as I did on honeymoon number one, I booked one night at a five-star hotel, Château Frontenac, with a breathtaking view of the St. Lawrence River. When we returned to Montreal, a sympathetic hotel clerk at the Laurentian saw a young couple in love and gave us a pass to keep the room throughout the convention.

Gene Alice was twenty-five; I was twenty-eight. We were one of the youngest couples at the convention. Introductions from senior members of the law firm enabled us to be included in formal closed sessions. We also were invited to join senior lawyers from major national firms for evening meals in five-star restaurants, restaurants we would never have found or been able to afford on our own. On the train back to Amarillo, Gene Alice leaned over to give me a kiss. "Being married to a successful lawyer is not so bad," she said.

Chapter Twenty-six

Gene Alice loved teaching at Palo Duro High School in Amarillo,. but teaching the same class year after year was not as challenging as her days as a student at the University of Wisconsin. She missed the intellectual stimulation of graduate school. I was made a partner in the law firm. Trial and appellate work changed case by case, so I enjoyed constant newness in my professional life. In other words, I was intellectually stimulated by work; Gene Alice, not so much. When she had told me she was coming home from Wisconsin at the end of her spring semester to make plans for our wedding, I knew that she would be short of her degree requirements. I promised her that I would do everything I could to help her finish. I contacted the University of Wisconsin's admissions office to determine what we needed to do. The university had a five-year rule that said all degree requirements must be completed on campus within five years. We had time, but we also had a deadline.

I still needed to fulfill my obligations to the army. Aside from that, we were eager to be active participants in our community. We joined the First Baptist Church and immediately were drafted to teach Sunday school to a class of junior high students, the boys in one room taught by me, the girls in the other room taught by Gene

Alice. She continued to take organ lessons from the organist at the Episcopal church and became the assistant organist at First Baptist, which prompted First Presbyterian to ask her to be an assistant organist there as well. It was just a block from the Baptist church. She also became an active member of the American Association of University Women. I went to every meeting of the young lawyer's club and spent weekends attending my army reserve unit as part of a multi-year requirement.

For fun, we joined the Twenty Thirty Club, which held regular dances, and we took up another hobby, bridge. Almost all of our older friends were serious bridge players. We signed up for lessons at the YWCA and then learned to play duplicate bridge at the Bridge House, a hall where serious players gathered in Amarillo.

We also got pregnant. We had barely been married a year. We both wanted children and were excited when Gene Alice returned from Dr. Lokey's office to say, "Max, we are going to have a baby. Let's keep it a secret until I start showing. I don't want our moms and friends to make a fuss." We attended the Texas Bar Association annual meeting in Houston and visited with an older lawyer friend and his wife, both high school classmates of my sister. Carolyn and Buddy Evans were the first to know we were going to have a baby, due in January 1963. Before we were back in Amarillo, the secret was out. It was almost time for Gene Alice to start showing. Now that we no longer had to keep it quiet, we signed up for Lamaze classes at Northwest Hospital, which our firm represented. Several of the other couples in the class became friends. We were faithful students, confident the classes would help Gene Alice handle the pain of childbirth and help me prepare to be her calm counselor. The classes did help, but not completely.

Well into our nine months of expectant-parenthood, we had tickets to hear Helen Hayes and Sir Laurence Olivier read works of Shakespeare. Our seats were on the first row of the balcony overlooking the stage. Midway through the performance, Gene Alice reached over to put my hand on her belly to feel the baby kicking and simply said, "I am about ready." We made it through a wonderful evening of Shakespearian theater, went home to pick up the bag of necessities Gene Alice had prepared weeks ago, and called Dr. Lokey to tell him it was time. Around midnight, we checked in at the hospital, and I helped Gene Alice put on her gown.

Dr. Lokey, an army-trained obstetrician-gynecologist, arrived and examined Gene Alice. "Mr. Sherman," he said, addressing me formally, despite being a client of our firm, "it will be several hours before this baby arrives. You can be with Mrs. Sherman in the labor room, but you will not be able to go in the delivery room. I will be sleeping on a cot down the hall and will check on her periodically."

A bevy of nurses and I were Gene Alice's Lamaze custodians. As I had been trained, I put my hand on her belly and held her hand and spoke soothingly or sang ditties. At one point when we were getting close, I had my hand on her belly and she cried out, "No, no, no. It is over there by Pakistan." I moved my hand. It was time for Dr. Lokey to take over and for me to take my seat in the waiting room.

It was a boy, Lynn Ray, born on January 30, 1963. We were thrilled and equally so twenty-three months later when our daughter, Holly Ruth, was born, December 15, 1964. Gene Alice was in love with motherhood, and I would have been happy with more children. But she had always wanted two, so we stopped there, and she immersed herself in nurturing our babies. By now the clock on completing her graduate degree was ticking loudly, and I had promised Gene Alice we would make sure she got her master's. Less than a year remained.

I fired off a letter to Madison to ask what we should do. An anonymous, but conscientious vice president in the admissions office called us. He said that her program required that she attend all classes on campus but that he had the authority to allow her to take the remaining courses in Texas. At the same time, he could not waive the requirement that she take her final oral exams in Madison. This smart, caring man then told us he would put the stipulations in a letter that Gene Alice should keep in case some other official had a different interpretation. The letter came. We kept it. For the next summer and the following semester, Genie enrolled in classes in nearby Canyon, at West Texas State University.

To coordinate classes that met the expectations of the University of Wisconsin-Madison and the Ford Foundation fellowship that funded her schooling, Gene Alice met with the head of the English department at West Texas State, Pat Sullivan. Dr. Sullivan supervised the liaison with UWM and agreed to let Gene Alice take three graduate courses that he taught. This was another serendipitous accident because, a few years later, he hired her to become a member of his faculty. The only hitch was, all of those classes were scheduled for eight o'clock in the morning. The university was sixteen miles from our home.

Genie was always a conscientious student: high school vale-dictorian, Phillips Petroleum Company Scholarship holder, taker of the most challenging courses, early to graduate, and, of course, a Ford Foundation Fellowship winner. It was difficult for her to study at home with two rambunctious children, so the solution was for her to drive to Canyon two hours before classes started to do her final preparation for the class ahead. That meant awakening about five in the morning, having breakfast, and starting her drive at 5:45. To make this work, we engaged a wonderful high school student, Robin Schroll, from our church. She arrived at our home at six o'clock. As the junior partner in the law firm, I had to fill in for court appearances for senior partners on vacation. Robin saved our lives that summer. I helped until I had to be in court, but she bathed, fed, and delivered the kids to their summer activities.

Gene Alice knocked out the top of her classes, which was no surprise to me. Her oral exams were scheduled in Madison. The kids, Robin, and I escorted her to the train station to board the overnight to Madison. This time, she did not carry a butcher knife for protection.

Chapter Twenty-seven

Our marriage continued a pattern of marking milestones every two years. Over the Christmas holidays, two years after Gene Alice got her graduate degree, she read a brief article in *Newsweek* about a program called the White House Fellows. Unknown to me, she sent off for the application. After thoroughly digesting it, she gave me a hug, saying, "You should apply for this." She went on to explain why I was the ideal applicant: a solid academic background, an elected student leader in high school and college, former president of the Texas Intercollegiate Student Association. "Texas is a big state," she added, "and there will not be many applicants who have that kind of credential. I would do it if I thought I had a chance, but few women are selected, and I don't have statewide experience."

She offered to help by editing my application and promptly handed it over. She studied my face as I read it. I turned to her. "Genie, I would love to do this, but I don't think it is possible. Five references are required, and one has to be from your present position." My law firm had made it clear from Day One that it wanted lawyers, not politicians. In my job interview, the partners asked me point blank if I harbored politician ambitions. I promised I had none. "This looks too much like politics," I said, handing the application back to Gene Alice.

"I thought of that," she said without a moment's hesitation. "Let's have dinner with Joe and Doris Harlan."

Joe was a named partner at the firm, and I worked closely with him. Doris was a dedicated librarian whom Gene Alice described as "the most outspoken, independent woman in Amarillo." They had no children, and Joe treated me like a son. Gene Alice was adamant we get their counsel before deciding whether to apply. As always, Joe's advice was what one would expect from one of the best trial lawyers in Texas — reasoned but blunt. "Almost all of the winners last year had one or more degrees from Ivy League schools. Your degrees are from Baylor and Texas. The odds are one hundred to one against you," he said. "I will be a reference, but for God's sake, don't tell anyone in the firm. They would fire both of us! If I don't do this, Doris will divorce me."

He might not have been joking. Doris had indeed weighed in during the discussion. "You have to give Gene Alice and Max this chance," she told Joe.

The Partnership relished the challenge of pulling together biographical material, deciding who the other four references would be, and, especially, submitting essays on a range of topics, including the big one, on world peace. I drafted the essay on why I was applying and why I thought I would be a good candidate and immediately turned it over to my editor, Gene Alice. At each stage of the competition, another essay was required. The Partnership collaborated and survived the occasional tussle over what to include, what to leave out, and what words sounded best. Then we waited. Soon, a letter appeared in the mailbox. I was a semi-finalist. One last essay was required, the one on world peace. Gene Alice leaned over to give me one of those I-told-you-so hugs.

"Do you remember that letter I wrote you from Texas City and signed, 'The Gay Philosopher?' As I recall, I counseled you that 'something which will be useful to me in some future dealing … will have its own string of consequences.' We wrote the Ross Essay on "World Peace Through Law" for the American Bar Association competition. It may be the key to this assignment on world peace. Let's revise it for this essay."

We were elated to learn soon thereafter that I had been chosen as one of thirty national finalists. A press release was sent to the *Amarillo Globe-News*. It ran it at the bottom of the front page and did not go unnoticed at the law firm. I was in trouble. Two of the senior partners demanded my immediate appearance on the office carpet, and the rest of the firm gathered. The opening consensus statement was just what I expected: "We want lawyers, not politicians."

"We have spent six years getting you ready to be a named partner," interjected another.

"How could you do this without telling us?"

Before I could mutter an explanation, Joe Harlan came to my rescue. "This publicity is good for the firm," he said brightly. "I've looked at the list of finalists, and Max is the only one without at least one Ivy League degree. He will not win. Let's cool down and let him go through the process and get this bee out of his bonnet."

Gene Alice and I quickly segued to trip-planning mode. The program would fly each finalist to Washington and then transport all thirty by bus, without our spouses, to a retreat center in rural Virginia. There, we would undergo five days of intensive interviews with panels made up of members of the White House Fellows board. They included some of the most prominent leaders in government, academia, and business: the editor of the New York Times editorial page; the president of the University of Colorado;

Olive Beach, head of her own aircraft manufacturing company; US Treasury Secretary Douglas Dillon, former head of the brokerage firm, Dillon Reed; and Judge William Hastie, a member of the US Court of Appeals for the Second Circuit and the first African American governor of the US Virgin Islands.

As always, Gene Alice was ahead of me. "Isn't Jay Taylor on that board?" she mused. "No, wait, I remember reading a recent news story that he is on one of the Rhodes Scholarship committees. You should call him and get his advice about these interviews." Taylor was a well-known Amarillo rancher and oil industry executive. I called him, and he invited me to come to his home before we flew to Washington. He looked over the list and said he served on the AT&T board with Douglas Dillon and would speak to him about me. "Where it may help is that it will cause him to pay attention when you are interviewed, rather than sit there picking his nose."

Taylor was a man of his word. On our first evening in Virginia, I went through a line to meet the board members. When I shook Douglas Dillon's hand he said, "Jay Taylor spoke to me about you."

At the White House function the following weekend, President Lyndon Johnson and Lady Bird hosted the finalists and their guests. Out of our meager bank account, we financed Gene Alice's expenses. As we arrived at the party, I was handed a note telling me that I was not one of the fifteen 1967 White House Fellows. Our disappointment was muted by the fact that we were dancing on the same floor with the President and First Lady. The Green Room was packed with celebrities. We were awestruck. California Congressman Bob Mathias, an American decathlete and two-time Olympic gold medalist, briefly took us under his wing.

"All of these people are professionals," he said. "If you see someone you want to meet, just go up to them. Tell them you have always wanted to meet them and introduce yourselves. That person will be flattered. You will have many interesting conversations."

We enthusiastically followed his advice. Gene Alice took the lead, meeting Supreme Court justices, senators, congressmen, members of the cabinet, and a host of Hollywood stars and business leaders we recognized from magazines, newspapers, and newsreels. She was in her element. We had total freedom to move from room to room. During a break in the action, we ventured into a hallway where a member of the final selection panel, Judge Hastie, called us aside. He assured us he was not violating any confidence by telling us that the panel originally was instructed to choose sixteen White House Fellows, but during the process, it was narrowed to fifteen. "Unfortunately, you were number sixteen," he said.

After we shared a few tears in private, Gene Alice and I continued exploring the hallway. We happened upon Walter Cronkite who introduced us to Secretary of Defense Robert McNamara. The secretary probably had not shaved since very early that morning. He carried a look of total exhaustion and a flat briefcase that looked as if it had been his companion since college. McNamara looked at my name tag and said, "Congratulations." I related what we had just learned from Judge Hastie. The secretary then told us his own story. "I missed being named a Rhodes Scholar by one notch. Had I been chosen, I would be teaching in some college today. It would have been a very different career. I would not have been president of Ford Motor Company and certainly not secretary of defense. Life often has a way of springing a string of unexpected blessings on you."

Chapter Twenty-eight

On the flight home, Gene Alice and I had a lot to talk about. Should I plunge in and become a full partner of the law firm, which brought with it prestige, country club membership, and several perks we had long ago rejected as our Partnership goals? Should she contact major universities and start chasing her longtime goal of earning a doctorate? Should I join the staff of a congressman or a senator so I could see politics from the inside? Wouldn't that give Genie more prestigious universities from which to choose? Wouldn't all but the first choices for each of us be like starting over? We had so many questions and so few answers. Our Southern Baptist heritage did tell us to pray about it.

As if an answer to prayer, I received a call three days later from Sargent Shriver's chief of staff. Shriver was the brother-in-law of Jack and Bobby Kennedy, a close friend of the Johnsons, and director of the recently created Office of Economic Opportunity, which had established several anti-poverty programs. Shriver had just read my White House Fellows file and wanted to interview me about becoming a member of his personal office staff. Could I come back to DC the day after tomorrow for the interview? The office would cover the cost of the flight and an overnight stay in a hotel. I knew Genie would say, "Yes, go for it," so I did, without hesitation. I told no one at the firm, not even Joe. That Thursday afternoon, I left work to catch a flight that got me into Washington by eleven o'clock that night. My interview appointment was at two o'clock Friday. I arrived thirty minutes early, but it was already too late.

"The director is at an important meeting at the White House," an assistant told me just before two o'clock. "He wanted me to assure you that he will be here as soon as possible." That scenario repeated itself at three, four, and five o'clock. I had several cups of coffee and several pieces of chocolate that aides kept offering me. At 5:30, the chief of staff told me Shriver was on his way. "Would you mind riding with him on his drive to his home? You will have the interview in the limousine."

Close to six o'clock that evening, I met this remarkable man. He found me in the waiting room. "Max, let's walk together for our ride to Virginia." We took off down a series of back hallways until we reached a private elevator. We exited to find a waiting limousine, larger than any car I had ever seen. We sat facing each other. He asked about my family and my Texas background. It was easy to see why he was so beloved by the Kennedys, the Johnsons, and almost everyone else who crossed his path. He had a captivating personality.

Almost an hour later, we arrived at his lovely Virginia home. As we drove up to the house, one of his sons appeared at the car window with a tennis racquet in hand. A father-son game had been scheduled for earlier that afternoon. I will never forget the sadness in Shriver's voice as he told his son he would quickly change and that they might be able to play a game or two. He was sorry, but there would be no time for more. As Shriver exited the limo, he told me the court was not lighted, and they had only about a half hour of daylight left. "If you don't mind, I'll hurry to the court. John will take you back to your hotel. We'll be in touch."

John, the chauffeur and trusted aide, knew why I was there. "Does this happen very often?" I asked him.

"Almost every day. His days are not his own. I pick up the mail from the office at 5:30 every morning and hand it to him when I arrive here. He signs and reads, works the phone, and when we get to his first appointment, I take the signed items to deliver to the appropriate staffer. The office calls me when it is time to drive him home or to another appointment. Often it is close to midnight before we head home."

I took an early morning flight back to Texas. That Saturday night, Gene Alice and I relived my Sargent Shriver experience. We both agreed that that was not a life we wanted for our young family. On Monday, when I got the call offering me the position, I told the chief of staff why I had to decline. She was very forthcoming in her reply. "We would love to work with you, but I think you are making the right decision. I don't have children so I can handle the almost twenty-four/seven schedule."

Gene Alice and I went back to the drawing board.

Chapter Twenty-nine

The law firm, unexpectedly, wrote the beginning of our next chapter, and it led with politics.

After the Texas legislative session ended in 1969, partner Erwin Ochsner and his wife, Burkella, hosted an outdoor summer party at their home. The firm's members were invited to help honor the Ochsners' closest friends of almost fifty years, Grady and Audrine Hazelwood. Grady had been a state senator for the thirty-first district since 1941. His Hazelwood Dairy was one of Erwin Ochsner's first major clients, and Burkella and Audrine were like sisters. These two strong women told Gene Alice the Hazelwoods had big plans — for me.

Audrine said that while her husband loved being a senator, he was thinking about not seeking re-election in 1970. Two or three state representatives were sending signals that they might challenge him, two in the Democratic primary and one Republican in the general election. "We can beat them, but it will mean several months of campaigning. We haven't had to do that for several years," Audrine told Gene Alice. "None of them should be in the senate."

Audrine went on to say that she and Grady realized the law firm would not support my getting into politics, but they thought the publicity I had gotten from the White House Fellows program, plus my Phillips pedigree, were a great combination. They believed I could win. "Grady will resign if Max decides to get in the race," Audrine confided. She added that it would be a tough race, but she promised she and Grady would work behind the scenes to help me get elected.

I was out of earshot for all of this but knew something was up. Gene Alice had a bounce in her voice and excitement in her eyes. We left the party, and she stayed upbeat during the car ride home. As soon as we walked into the living room, she said, "Let's sit down and talk. I have the best news. I know it is an answer to our prayers about what do we do next." She told me everything Audrine had said. "I think we should give it a shot. I can't do it because I am a woman. But you can."

Sadly, she was right. Women were longshot candidates for Texas voters. Since the 1920s, few women had been elected to the state legislature. Just one woman was in the thirty-one-member senate; less than a handful served in the 150-member house. The Panhandle district that Grady represented was considered the most conservative in Texas. Gene Alice was a big believer in women's rights, but she was matter-of-fact about the unfairness of women's election prospects. We both knew she had great political qualities, and if the times — and the makeup of our senatorial district had been different — she would have been elected easily and would have been an outstanding state senator. I believe she also would have been a strong contender for a higher office. She had made clear before we married that she would not live her dreams *through* me. Instead, she would live them *with* me, as a full partner, just as she functioned in our marriage every day and in my law career.

"I will go to the library and check out every book on how to get elected," she said, brightly. "You can run your traps for resources within the Democratic Party."

Getting into politics had been in the back of my mind since college. The White House Fellows program had given me a tiny taste of political life, and I realized I loved policy and had great admiration for the public servants who sought solutions to society's most vexing problems. Now, my political aspirations were taking shape. I really had Gene Alice to thank for this. She was nothing but encouraging. I kept saying to myself and often out loud, "That's Gene Alice, she's one hell of a woman!"

She was thirty-one, and I was thirty-four. Our children were in elementary school. "You know, this will be the straw that breaks the camel's back," I told her. "If we do this, I will have to go to another firm or practice law by myself. It's a big risk. Our young family will be in limbo."

As always, she was a step ahead of me. "I don't think so. With Burkella's quiet support and with Erwin and Joe's affection for you, I think the firm will let you run because they will be convinced we can't win." She went on to say she knew I loved practicing law but couldn't stop thinking about our days at Baylor, sitting together on the quad and watching my excitement when the topic turned to politics.

"I have watched the political fuse slowly burn, as you gradually got more and more involved in Democratic Party politics, as we put together the material for the White House Fellows, as we worked the crowd in the White House, as we watched President and Mrs. Johnson dance, as I watched you look into the eyes of Secretary McNamara and Judge Hastie. This is our chance to do something important beyond the courthouse and the classroom."

Gene Alice was all in, but the law firm decidedly was not. When I told the managing partner I intended to enter the race for the Texas Senate seat held by Grady Hazelwood, he was irate.

A meeting of all twenty-three members of the firm was called that night. I made my pitch and was asked to leave. I went down to my office and wrote an order to sell all of the only stock we owned. If we had to leave the firm, we could live off the proceeds for a few months. After that, we would be back where we were on Cheyenne Terrace, in love but broke. As Gene Alice predicted the vote was overwhelmingly against our running, twenty 'nos' to three 'yeses.' But they weren't kicking me out yet. On Joe's recommendation, the partners agreed to let me continue in my job for the duration of the election. If I lost, I could return to the firm with a promise that politics was out of my blood. If we won, the firm would meet and decide what our relationship would be.

Chapter Thirty

The Partnership cranked up. Gene Alice and our friend Joanne consumed books on politics. I did the legal work to determine how to proceed. A candidate had to register in each of the district's twenty counties, either by mail or in person. With help from our moms to take care of our children, Gene Alice and I set out on a road trip to visit every county in the district and file papers in the homes of each Democratic Party chair, nineteen men and one woman. The area covered a wide swath of West Texas with a population of 600,000, which, in those days, was larger than the populations of five states. It would take many days to cover all twenty counties, and we'd return home to our children very late each night so they'd see us in the morning before we did it all over again.

Not one of the party chairs could recall a time when a candidate filed in person in each county, and certainly, none could recall any being accompanied by his wife. Normally, I'd say *spouse,* but none remembered a woman ever filing for the seat. In almost every visit, I handled the paperwork with the chair, and Gene Alice made friends with the spouse. The lone woman was the Collingsworth County chair, who was known as Momma Coleman. She loved Gene Alice, and after a much longer visit than usual, Coleman said she had to be neutral in the primary but pledged to do everything in her power to help us get elected if I became the nominee.

We were so naive. We had no money and no professional political advice, other than a handbook from the National Democratic Committee. Our foot soldiers were all amateurs — family and friends who offered to help. But despite our inexperience, we never doubted that we just might win. Gene Alice was at my side for every event: walking the local parade routes in almost every county seat, attending all of the volunteer firefighter cookouts, dancing at every barn dance. She was always working the crowds with me, even in enemy territory. I could not have done it without her, and I'm sure voters got the idea: When they chose me, they also chose my indefatigable, politically astute partner.

The first big political event was at the Pipefitter's Union Hall where husbands and wives sat for the speeches. I had been told that there was no way labor would support us because I was a partner in a big law firm that represented many of the workers' employers. So, we decided to walk side by side, row by row, and meet and greet each member. It was our introduction to learning to work the floor and tables. Gene Alice is convinced that many of those labor wives silently voted for us. We made several lifelong friends.

When we were not on the road, Gene Alice and Joanne put together lists of friends and family scattered throughout the district, along with their telephone numbers. As each person on the list was called, Genie and Joanne urged them to vote and get all of their family and friends to do the same. We kept the list of phone numbers. I would need them to mount a successful run.

In the May 2, 1970, primary, we came in second. The runoff was one month later, on June 6. Our team of volunteers called all of the numbers we had gathered and turned out a resounding victory. Gene Alice and Joanne became my general election co-chairs. They made calls using the same lists, and a high percentage of our supporters turned out at the polls that November 3. We won.

Chapter Thirty-one

M y use of the pronouns *we* and *our* is intentional. I was the partner who voted in the Texas Senate, gave floor speeches, and chaired the Senate Natural Resources Committee, but Gene Alice was an equal partner every moment we served, from 1971 to 1977. She was my confidante and adviser in every big decision a senator must make. We spoke at least once a day on the phone. She met with constituents, campaigned with me, planned our strategy. Two historic events defined our tenure: a bank fraud scandal that ensnared state leaders and our number one agenda item, passing the Equal Rights Amendment.

Out of 181 Texas state lawmakers in 1971, only two were women, Sissy Farenthold, a Corpus Christi Democrat, in the House, and Barbara Jordan, a Houston Democrat, in the senate. I was among four new senators joining the thirty-one-member body in January 1971. We drew lots to determine seniority. I was number twenty-eight. Under normal circumstances, it would take ten or more years to become senate president, but the Sharpstown Bank Scandal was starting to play out. It involved the big three in Texas government: Governor Preston Smith, Lieutenant Governor Ben Barnes, and House Speaker Gus Mutscher. Houston developer and banker Frank Sharp had offered the officials a generous loan to buy shares in one of his companies, thus inflating the stock value. The officials could then sell off the stock and keep the proceeds, provided they passed a few advantageous banking bills Sharp wanted. Whispers of a quid pro quo reached a crescendo in 1971 when the feds opened an investigation. I took office as the shadow of impropriety hung over legislative leaders. It was also a redistricting session, which meant that all members of the legislature, even those elected to four-year terms, had to be on the ballot in 1972. Fortunately, Gene Alice and I had previously defeated all of our likely opponents. We did not have a contested race in the primary or the general election, an election that brought seventy-eight new members to the 150-member state house and sixteen new state senators. Number twenty-eight suddenly became number one to be elected senate president under a new lieutenant governor. I would also continue chairing my committee, which pretty much had the economy of Texas in its hands.

The ERA did not move as swiftly through the legislature as the fallout from the Sharpstown scandal. In every legislative session throughout the late 1950s and 1960s, an amendment was introduced to give women equal rights with men. All failed. The American Association of University Women was a fierce champion of amending the constitution to give equal rights to women, and that was yet another reason Genie was an active member. In the 1971 session, Barbara Jordan introduced and passed, with our "aye" vote, an ERA to amend the Texas Constitution. On March 22, 1972, the Congress passed and sent to the states a federal ERA, and the Texas Legislature met in a special session on March 30, 1972, to ratify it. That November, seventy-nine percent of Texas voters approved the ERA. We had been part of something important. For Genie, it was also personal. Some years later, she would give a speech in Amarillo on why she believed so vehemently in the ERA.

"A final barrier to equality is our lack of a sense of power," she told the Distinguished Women's Service Awards program in 1988. "Women have not yet dared enough. We need to think for ourselves. We need to speak out. We need to trust our intuition. To rely on our own strength and resilience, to be women of consequence, existing on our own terms, savvy and powerful individuals ... And who needs powerful women? Religion, politics, law enforcement, business, the arts, journalism, medicine, advertising, manufacturing, social services, government, industry."

In that speech and at other times, Gene Alice expressed her admiration for three first ladies: Lady Bird Johnson "for making the world beautiful wherever she goes," Betty Ford, who "communicated how women are especially vulnerable to drugs and alcohol," and Rosalynn Carter for "her vision and her strength to tackle big problems like world health, housing, and hunger."

"Each of them could have been in the shadow of her husband," Genie told her Amarillo audience, "but each of them shines. not with a reflected light, but with a presence and power that is her own."

Chapter Thirty-two

The Partnership was sound but rowing into choppy waters. Politics had become an addiction, especially for me. Because all Texas senators were on the ballot in 1972, Genie and I were very lucky not to attract an opponent. Those elected in 1972 drew lots to determine who had two-year terms and who had four-year terms. We drew four years, a blessing and a curse. As a conservative Democrat serving as president of the senate, we were under considerable pressure to run for Congress in 1974, a seat held by a Republican for eight years. The district now leaned Democratic, and we were being encouraged by business and political leaders on both sides of the aisle to go after it.

"We can almost guarantee that you will not have an opponent in either party. At least, we will not support any serious candidate," they assured us. The political addiction hardened when they added, "It might be a stepping stone to the United States Senate or governor."

We knew to be cautious about pursuing a career in Washington, DC. Recalling the day I witnessed Sargent Shriver disappointing his son about playing tennis and hearing the sadness in Shriver's voice, made the proposal less seductive. But I had to give it serious thought. So, after the 1973 session ended, we loaded our Ford station wagon and took our young children to the nation's capital to verify our deeply felt hunch that we should decline. Barbara Jordan, who remained a close friend and had fallen in love with our children, came to our rescue. Over apple pie à la mode in a congressional dining room, she gave us tremendously helpful advice.

"I am single. I have no children. From our first meeting you included me in your family. I would love to have you here as a colleague. God knows we need you, but in my one term, I've watched ruined marriages. My advice would be to stay in the Texas Senate. You can do more good as one of thirty-one than to cool your heels for ten or twelve years to have the same influence among 435."

When we returned to Amarillo, I called my good friend and fellow state senator, Jack Hightower, another West Texas conservative Democrat. "Jack, Gene Alice and I are not going to enter the race for Congress. I know you want to run. We will help you get elected. In fact, we will host your first event at our home in Amarillo." He was elected and held the seat for ten years.

I focused on my work in the senate, which grew increasingly demanding. Gene Alice, meanwhile, wore a slew of hats back home. She loved being a university English professor and the organist at the First Presbyterian Church. Aside from her commitment to her family, those were her two highest priorities. She was managing our home in Amarillo almost singlehandedly. We wondered if it would make sense to have two family homes — one in Austin, the other in Amarillo so we could all be together more. Our children strenuously opposed the idea. They did not want to leave their friends in Amarillo. We decided the family would stay in Amarillo and I would continue my commute, catching the Monday morning flight to Austin at 6:20 and returning for weekends whenever I could. We soldiered through the 1974 Constitutional Convention and the 1975 session and were re-elected to a new four-year term in 1976, again without opposition.

As part of the leadership, I was expected to serve on most, if not all, of the controversial conference committees to work out differences between the house and senate versions of legislation. Many weekends I slept on a mattress on the floor of an apartment rented by Bob Simpson, one of our state representatives. I rarely made it home on the weekends. After six years of this, I not only was exhausted, I was lonely for my family. The fissures in the Partnership got bigger, reminding me of an ice skater who is warned: "If you see a fissure in the ice on a frozen lake, you'll want to take off your skates and head back to the car." Was it time for me to head back to the car?

Gene Alice made me see it. "Max, the Texas Senate is no different than Washington, DC. You are never home. I am now a house mum. The children need you. I need you. This is not working."

In desperation, I came up with one of the most helpful responses of my life. "You are so right. I am miserable. You are miserable. The children are frustrated. Why don't you and Joanne James plan a trip to the wine country in Europe for Paul and Joanne and you and me?"

Just before we left, U. S. Senator Lloyd Bentsen asked if he could recommend me for a federal district judgeship. With our good friends, we would have time away from home to consider life after elective politics.

Chapter Thirty-three

The Shermans and the Jameses closed down a five-star Indonesian restaurant in Amsterdam debating my future. My options appeared to be: accepting an appointment to a federal judgeship, joining a big law firm, or simply staying in the state senate. The head waiter hesitantly but pointedly asked us to leave. "Sir, it is very late."

We all agreed that none of those choices would serve the Partnership's Wisconsin Plan. Gene Alice and I had to be equal partners, each respecting the other's opportunities. We were each other's strength as we always had been, in the same way we discussed books, movies, and plays. After returning to our small hotel we continued our confessional, but we did not have a priest to administer a blessing and forgiveness. There was no easy answer.

As we traipsed through the wine country of France and Germany, it was an intermittent topic of our four-way conversations. Rarely did I call home when trying to get away from the day-to-day demands of my job, but Governor Dolph Briscoe had threatened to call a third special session of the Texas Legislature. I needed to get an update and called my office. Texas Smith, my right arm at my law practice and the chief of staff in my senate office, answered. "I'm so glad you called," she said. "The governor is not calling the special session until end of the summer, but here is something you have to worry about. Someone has nominated you to be president of West Texas State University. I've told the press I do not know how to contact you, but when you return, they will be waiting for you at the airport." We now had a fourth option to discuss as we left Paris for our final days in London.

We chose higher education. I stepped down from the senate in 1977 for the top job at West Texas State University, based in Canyon, the middle of the Panhandle. Genie remained a professor there, and we would find that we loved the presidency even more than the senate. Important legislation touches the lives of many people, but it's not visceral or personal. The role of a regional university president gives you day-to-day contact with faculty and students and many opportunities to give talks and even commencement speeches to local high school students. The personal contact is constant and stimulating. I found it much more satisfying than lawmaking. Best of all, my family and I were together again. Gene Alice and I could entertain again. We would both be parents to our two children together. Genie, the professor, Max, the president. The Partnership was entering a new phase.

Chapter Thirty-four

After five wonderful, creative years leading a regional university, I realized I wasn't done with politics. The addiction was back, for me, along with heavy political pressure. Gene Alice wasn't feeling the pull because she remembered my time in the senate all too clearly. It was 1982, a year Democrats were expected to sweep all of the statewide elective offices in Texas. My choice for attorney general, Senator Ray Farabee, called and said that for family and personal reasons, he could not make the race. "It is essential to have a West Texas conservative Democrat on the ticket. You have to do it."

Genie was ambivalent about me running, which should have sounded an alarm. We loved the academic life, but she knew me. If the political bug was still biting, we had to swat it away or kill it by taking a longshot chance on winning a statewide office that might keep us in politics for the rest of our lives. The minus column was longer than the plus side. Against our better judgment, we joined the Democratic primary. The fuse was too short. Not enough time to mount a campaign in a state so vast. Not enough money. No way to campaign as a team. One partner went one way, the other partner went the other. We were never together. We lost. Fortunately.

As Secretary McNamara had said when he met us — that life had brought him a "string of unexpected blessings" — so it was for me. Because of the statewide visibility I had gained from the attorney general campaign, the search committee for dean of the Lyndon B. Johnson School of Public Affairs asked to consider me for the Austin-based, University of Texas job. All of the conversations we had with Joanne and Paul in Europe pointed us in the direction of saying yes. If I were chosen, Gene Alice would be in Austin and could finish her doctorate.

I also had an invitation to serve as special counsel to the newly elected governor, Democrat Mark White. I didn't hesitate to say yes. This would give us an income while the intensive, national search for a dean ensued. Genie was able to continue for a semester at West Texas State and be a single parent for our daughter, who was wrapping up her last year of high school. Our lives seemed to be falling neatly into place as if by design, rather than being influenced by "almosts." Almost winning the Ross Essay competition, almost being named a White House fellow, almost winning the Democratic primary for attorney general. Each "almost" had opened another door.

I was named dean in 1983. Gene Alice moved to Austin. Both of our children were at Vanderbilt. Genie began her coursework at the University of Texas, and while still doing that, in 1987, she was unexpectedly asked to become director of UT's Thompson Conference Center, which not only hosts events on campus but puts on continuing educational programs for adults. She accepted and had free rein to create new programs and did, including travel abroad for older adults, continuing education for those over fifty-five, computer training, and language skills learning. At forty-nine, she would lead her own university. She loved being in charge and seeing lives being transformed and revitalized by learning.

We were intensely busy but settling into a comfortable middle age. Throughout our years in leadership roles at the University of Texas, and in retirement, we kept up a favorite pastime: We entertained at home, lavishly by some standards. We had built our home on Greenway Street, just north of the university, in 1983 with entertaining embedded in the design. Our holiday parties extended over five nights in early December when we entertained different groups on different nights, including colleagues from UT, friends from church, political contacts, business friends and neighbors. After we retired, we pared back the guest list slightly but still needed four nights of parties. Genie planned the menus, did the invitation lists, hired the musicians, and coordinated everything. I made sure the wood floors were polished, the light fixtures decorated, and the windows cleaned. It was so much fun. After a full four nights in December 2002, having entertained hundreds of friends and family members, we slumped on the sofa beside one another, took off our shoes, and toasted each other with a glass of wine. Then Gene Alice leaned into my shoulder, gave me a kiss on the cheek, and said the words that shook me like no others: "Max, for the first time in my life, I felt overwhelmed. I think I need to see a doctor."

The monster was on the doorstep, and I hadn't even noticed.

ACT III

Chapter Thirty-five

My first thoughts were cancer, heart disease, or a brain aneurysm. Nothing else made sense. My partner performed at 1,000 percent in everything she did. Always had. If she felt overwhelmed, surely something physically debilitating was occurring. Yet, there were no outward signs. A few days later, on New Year's Eve, forty-three years after our first New Year's Eve babysitting and discussing T. S. Eliot, Gene Alice opened up to me with a vulnerability that was, frankly, frightening.

"As a little girl, and even through our first year of marriage, I watched my grandfather deteriorate from a Bible-quoting, pulpit-pounding preacher to a docile, silent presence at big family gatherings," she began. "He could not quote Scripture from memory or recall events of his life or even engage in conversation, even though some core deep inside of him insisted that he always wear a suit with a pressed shirt and a well-chosen tie. Recently, I've started forgetting things that were always at the front of my mind: phone numbers, locations, names of friends' children and spouses. I thought it was just being too busy and pushing too hard, but it hasn't gone away. During our Thanksgiving break, I slipped off to the library and read a couple of articles about dementia and Alzheimer's. In between, I've been listening to the DVD by

Norman Cousins on positive emotions and health. I may not have it, but I need to know. I'm terrified to even think I might end up like my grandfather."

I couldn't believe what I was hearing. I knew that memory could slip as a natural part of aging, but Genie was surely going overboard with this. She was only sixty-four, too young for Alzheimer's or dementia, unless it was the early-onset variety. I had read that worry about memory can make normal forgetting worse. Clearly, my brilliant wife just needed reassurance. So, I tried, but that wasn't enough. She wanted professional help, and I did not want to argue or become an obstacle. If I had learned anything in my four-plus decades with Gene Alice, it was to get the hell out of the way when her mind was made up.

Chapter Thirty-six

The Center for BrainHealth, established in 1999 at the University of Texas at Dallas, was suddenly on our places-we've-never-been-but-must-visit list. The center combines brain research and clinical interventions and was the best option close to Austin for a memory assessment. Our son-in-law, Carlos, was a vice-president at the university and arranged an appointment for Gene Alice to go in late-January 2003 for an intensive evaluation.

I was terrified — afraid to say a word that might add to Gene Alice's concern and scared not to say something that would let her know how much I cared. Outwardly, I was the calm, reassuring husband. If Gene Alice had the stage to tell her version, I'm sure she would say, "Max was always so transparent. I was the one who did the reassuring. On the road to Dallas for my appointment, I told him, 'Max, I just want to know what's going on.'"

After we checked in at the center, we had an orientation interview with Sandra Bond Chapman, the founder and chief director. We were given the chance to respond to Dr. Bond's many questions. It was now time for Gene Alice to go through a series of tests, without my being present. For what seemed like an eternity, I sat alone in the corner of a hallway. I noticed a bronzed plaque identifying the center's major founding donors.

The name T. Boone Pickens jumped out. Boone was a friend and former law firm client with whom I had once played an hour of racquetball each week. I took a chance on calling him, knowing that since he had become so famous in the business world, I might not be able to get through a maze of assistants. After speaking with the receptionist, he took my call. Boone told me why he was so passionate about the center. As a longtime physical fitness buff, he realized as he aged that mental fitness was equally important. He asked me to give him my evaluation of how well the center worked with Gene Alice and let him know if we needed anything. I don't recall ever asking for his help, but it was nice being reassured by a friend.

Two days of testing confirmed that Gene Alice was smart. Her abstract reasoning and her ability to integrate ideas and concepts were in the upper percentile. Her general memory was solid. The tests did indicate some difficulty maintaining attention and concentration. In the exit interview, Dr. Chapman said the results showed no immediate concern because Genie performed at such a high level. But because Gene Alice was concerned and because of her slight difficulty in maintaining focus, Dr. Chapman recommended that she return for an updated evaluation, if her concerns persisted.

As the lawyer in the Partnership, I took the report as a verdict that "all is well, not guilty." I was happy not to worry. The English professor partner took it as literature to be examined carefully for nuances. She started keeping a journal.

Chapter Thirty-seven

Although we were several years into retirement, we did not retire from life. We rarely missed a performance of the symphony or the opera. We continued to travel with our Dallas friends: two cruises on the Baltic and one land and water excursion on the St. Lawrence River that took us through parts of Canada and New England. Each summer we escaped the heat in Austin and spent several weeks at a rural summer home we bought in Livingston, Montana, about a half-hour away from Bozeman.

Genie remained as passionate as ever about music. She sang in the University Presbyterian Church Choir in Austin, which meant a two-hour practice session on Wednesday nights and early-to-church on Sundays for an abbreviated practice, followed by the morning service. Genie loved to play the piano with our Scottie, Olive, sitting beside her bench, eyes fixed on the performer. Our two grown children were married and had settled in Texas, one in Austin, the other in Dallas after a two-year stint in Mexico City. We were active grandparents for our six granddaughters: two sets of identical twins in son Lynn's family and two who are citizens of Mexico and the United States in Holly's family. Not a bad life.

On Easter Sunday 2006, midway through the pastor's sermon, Genie put her head on my shoulder and promptly fainted. Friends

sitting in the pews around us helped me get her out of the sanctuary. As we walked down the aisle, her head still pressed into my
shoulder, she quickly recovered and resisted going to a doctor or a
hospital. She kept insisting, "I'm alright. I'm alright." We wrote off
the episode to Genie getting overheated or being overly tired, but it
scared our kids. Even though it was not her birthday, they planned a
belated sixty-eighth birthday party in June that would make it easier
for friends from Amarillo and around the state to come to Austin to
celebrate. Her brother and his wife came from New York City, several
friends came from Amarillo, and many from her former job at UT
and from church showed up. The festivities had barely begun when
she fainted. I was going to be delayed arriving at the party because
I was at a meeting in South Austin. Her brother, Carl, and our son,
Lynn, rushed her to an emergency room at a local hospital. Holly
called my cellphone, alerting me to meet them there. Genie's inter-
nist and the cardiologist who was called to consult on her condition
concluded that she needed a pacemaker to regulate an abnormally
low heartbeat. That was what had caused her fainting spells.

The pacemaker was implanted under general anesthesia, but
the procedure took much longer than what we had been told. In
the past, whenever a loved one or close friend was in the hospital,
Gene Alice and I would sit in the waiting room and fret together.
But now Gene Alice was the patient, leaving the other half of the
Partnership to worry alone. Eventually, the cardiologist appeared
and told me there had been "a few complications." Because she was
in such good physical health it took longer to make the connection
to the heart. I did not understand the significance of her being
under anesthesia that long, but he assured me that all had gone
well. To my knowledge, Genie had been in the hospital only three
times in her life, to have her appendix removed as a teenager and to

have two children. I was probably in denial and did not notice any change in Genie, but Holly later told Dr. Hart at the BrainHealth Center that she had "observed a noticeable change in her memory performance."

After the surgery, I went to Genie's room. Not surprisingly, she was smiling and held up her head for a kiss. That summer, we spent two months in Montana, taking several all-day float trips on the Yellowstone River and one five-day trek with a guide on the Missouri River. Gene Alice was a super trout angler. Just below the dam on the Missouri, at 5:30 in the morning, fishing from the front of the boat, she pulled in several eighteen-to-twenty-one-inch rainbows. There were four or five other fishing boats in the area, but she was the only angler catching fish. All summer she had no problems performing tasks or remembering. We chugged along.

Chapter Thirty-eight

Amid the Christmas cards that arrived in our mailbox in 2006 was a reminder to schedule a follow-up session at the Center for BrainHealth. I'm sure Genie was faithfully keeping her journal, but I didn't see anything to worry about. "Do you want to schedule another session at the BrainHealth Center?" I asked her.

She didn't hesitate. "Oh, yes. The center is building a baseline to evaluate me if there are any future complications. This is like a six-month dental appointment to get your teeth cleaned and checked to see if there are any cavities." She wouldn't dream of canceling.

On April 27, 2007, Genie took a battery of tests under the direction of Jennifer Zientz, head of clinical services. Jennifer was not concerned by what she saw, and no diagnosis was made. She would compare the test results with Gene Alice's 2003 report and get back to us. When she did, Genie took notes. The report was not at all worrisome but contained several general recommendations: Continue journaling about family and fun things; play the piano and go to art galleries and museums; avoid multi-tasking; and, she underlined, exercise your intact abilities. Because nearly four years had passed since the initial evaluation, Jennifer scheduled an October appointment with Dr. John Hart Jr., medical science director.

Our daughter, Holly, went with us. Dr. Hart was pleased that some of Gene Alice's scores were quite good. He complimented her on her impeccable appearance and her ability to joke with him. She was comfortable with Dr. Hart and admitted to him that, despite her appearance, she had "lots of anxiety." He reassured us, saying that "very smart people are more at risk for this than others because they are used to functioning at such a high level."

Holly took notes. We braced ourselves for the bad news we felt was coming next.

"Dr. Hart said he eliminated frontal lobe problems by observation," Holly wrote. "She entered the room with confidence, with me behind her. She shook hands with everyone, is put together in dress, stands straight, and sits calmly in a chair. She took control. He said that she appears like a working woman but that she needs to have fun, too."

Then, the clincher. "Dr. Hart diagnosed Mild Cognitive Impairment (MCI). Though she experiences some deficiencies, she is able to compensate and is very sharp, and her deficiencies are not significantly disrupting her life. He said that this eliminates the diagnosis of dementia."

But MCI is like a bridge that leads to a fork in the road. One path takes the traveler to normal memory decline consistent with aging. The other path leads to dementia or, worse yet, Alzheimer's. I was worried but not alarmed. Gene Alice seemed to be functioning quite well and enjoying life. Besides, she was my right arm. No, she was much more than that. She was the love of my life and truly the heart of the Partnership. She kept me grounded in reality but unafraid to dream. She made life sweet, worth getting out of bed in morning. It was her voice I heard speaking in my mind, and sometimes I couldn't tell where her voice ended and mine began. If this was the worst of it, then it wasn't so bad, I decided.

But I noticed she had been growing more anxious. She had admitted to Holly's husband, Carlos, that she wasn't trying as hard to communicate with others at social gatherings. After Holly passed this on to Dr. Hart in front of Genie, he responded beautifully. He took Genie's hand, looked in her eyes, and told her that it was very important to stay engaged and active. "Since groups can be hard, grab someone for a one-on-one visit," he said, gently. "Keep doing dinner parties. I don't want you to change a thing — except worry less."

He then warned us about the importance of avoiding general anesthesia. "When a person is in the ballpark of a memory problem, going under general can make it worse." He advised us to call him first if Gene Alice should face surgery, unless, of course, it was an emergency. He wanted to see if there might be a way for her to avoid general anesthesia. The notion of anesthesia exacerbating dementia was still speculative, but Dr. Hart said he had seen enough to believe in being cautious. Indeed, studies going back to 1998 suggested that anesthesia can worsen dementia because it activates receptors in the brain for memory loss so patients don't remember traumatic experiences during surgery. But for some people, the memory loss endures.

"Why, oh, why did we not have this meeting before the pacemaker?" I wondered. We had had no idea this could be a problem.

Before we left that day, Dr. Hart recommended a half-dozen behavioral modifications to help Gene Alice cope with MCI on a daily basis. She should stop multitasking and focus on one task at a time, dedicating uninterrupted time each day to returning phone calls and responding to emails. She needed to spend time doing the things she truly enjoyed, such as playing the piano, creating art, and visiting museums. She should develop a strategy to address people whose names she was having trouble remembering, such as calling people "friend," rather than worrying about forgetting. She could reduce her anxiety by developing a daily routine to support memory and help maintain independence. As much as she might not like it, she should recruit help to minimize stress with such tasks as cooking, cleaning, shopping, and driving. And she should keep journaling to exercise her brain, focusing on favorite life experiences rather than on anxiety-inducing events.

The whole time Dr. Hart was with us, he was teaching. Two interns were in the room with Genie, along with a resident who was assisting Dr. Hart on a dementia study. They were learning by observing her appearance, reactions, and responses. A funny moment occurred during the two-hour session when Dr. Hart asked Genie if she smoked crack to see how she would react. "Certainly not," she retorted.

His final recommendation was to make an appointment for her to have a brain scan at the Austin Neurological Center. He did not want to alarm her but wanted to rule out other possibilities for her continuing memory lapses. A diagnostic radiologist and partner of Dr. Hart's read the CT scan. It was normal. She had no tumor that would impair her memory, no aneurysm, no sign of a stroke. Dr. Hart asked us to come back once a year for a follow-up and set our next appointment December 7 and 8, 2008.

Genie incorporated Dr. Hart's recommendations into her daily life. She suggested that we join the duplicate bridge club from our church and buy a Nintendo hand-held game device so that we could play together at home. To my surprise, she even asked if she could join me on my early-morning jogs. Wow! She was taking charge, once again. Thanks to a changed lifestyle, she continued performing at a high level. Even so, the disease continued its dirty work.

Chapter Thirty-nine

Back at the Center for BrainHealth on December 7, 2008, Jennifer Zientz conducted tests similar to the ones done fourteen months earlier. Our diligent notetaker Holly was with us again and was asked what she had detected in the past year. Genie's short-term memory loss was more pronounced than a year ago, Holly said. Oddly, her mother didn't acknowledge having any difficulty with memory, despite being asked several different ways. It was as if, ironically, she had forgotten about it.

The next day, Gene Alice saw Dr. Hart, who after a brief light-hearted exchange, asked her what was going on. She answered that she was doing very well and that was about it, thank you very much. Holly joked that her mother remained an optimist, so he asked Holly what she thought. She repeated what she had said a day earlier to Jennifer, that Genie's memory loss was worsening. Dr. Hart confirmed that the testing had shown that, too, and that given the sharp decline in memory over the past year, he said she was on the edge between Mild Cognitive Impairment and Mild Alzheimer's. He diagnosed her with both, leaving no doubt where the MCI was heading. He asked Genie if she was depressed, and she acknowledged feeling blue at times, something she said she was embarrassed to admit. From a physiological perspective, Dr.

Hart explained that the neurons that fire for depression are in close proximity to those in the memory center, so the two conditions often are seen in tandem. And the neurons that fire for depression also fire for anxiety, so those also often go hand in hand. Because mild depression can worsen memory, Dr. Hart said addressing Genie's depression could help her memory.

She had been taking Lexapro for anxiety, and Dr. Hart recommended doubling the dose. He added Namenda and Aricept, two drugs for dementia that won't stop the progression but might help nonetheless. He also urged physical exercise — walking at least three times a day, enrolling in the Alzheimer's Center in Dallas so she could receive the newest drugs, continuing a healthy diet, and getting eight hours of sleep nightly.

Genie read and re-read Holly's notes and the written report the center provided. Always the good student, she studied her mental condition in much the same way she would prepare for a class on Shakespeare or Hemingway.

Our friends Tom and Judy invited us to join them for dinner at Genie's favorite Mexican restaurant. Judy knew that Genie was concerned about her memory because shortly after the December 2008 meeting with Dr. Hart, Genie had confided to her. "I know that if my memory keeps slipping away, Max will take care of me. But I don't want him to have to do that." I was not surprised when Judy told me that Gene Alice had said she didn't want me to "have to" take care of her, but she knew I was in this with her. Thirty-five years earlier, when I first started commuting from Amarillo to Austin, I learned that even in times of separation, we would always take care of each other. We relied on one another and celebrated the unique qualities that made our partner the one we wanted to be with the most, in good times and in bad.

Judy used our dinner out together as an opportunity to help her lifelong friend. She talked about how she and Tom had decided to move to a senior retirement community and had been scouting out three different options in the Austin area. Judy planted the seed that led to our eventual move to one of the communities she glowingly described. "I think you guys should look into this."

Genie and I visited the marketing department of all three and took tours of the available apartments. She was emphatic that two were "too far away. We would be isolated if we moved there." That's how we chose Westminster Manor, a retirement community that spans independent living to skilled nursing and memory care, with a large campus in the heart of Austin. It was close to almost all of our activities. Plus, the complex was expanding with new apartments opening soon. And, so in June 2009, we put our name on the priority list, made an initial deposit, and started going to the "let's get acquainted" events where we met several longtime friends who lived there. We never missed a session that was aimed at preparing us for the emotional and practical implications of moving out of a much-loved home of many years.

We continued to live the good life, but I soon realized the monster was no longer standing outside the door. It had slipped inside our home and was taking what it wanted.

Chapter Forty

Genie continued to sing in the choir and drive herself to practice. But then she started hitching a ride with a friend. On Sunday mornings, the friend would take her to the abbreviated practice, and then after the service, Genie and I would leave together in my car to have lunch with friends. I had quietly observed how this change in habit had started, with Gene Alice calling the shots.

It started one Wednesday evening after practice. Genie forgot where she had parked. As she stood outside the parking garage looking bewildered, Carolyn, a friend in the choir who happened to be walking by, took Genie by the hand and walked with her. They would get in Carolyn's car and drive around until they saw Gene Alice's car, but as it happened, Carolyn had parked next to Genie. Gene Alice was so rattled by the experience that she never again drove herself to choir practice. Carolyn became her chauffeur, and not long after she started driving her, Carolyn called to tell me that Genie was no longer able to stand during the entire two-hour practice. The choir director suggested that she stay seated, but that was unacceptable to Genie. If she were going to sing, she would do it like everyone else. It was not her style to accept preferential treatment. And if she could no longer stand, then she'd simply quit.

Carolyn fully expected that to be Gene Alice's next move. "Max, this is just a heads-up," she said. That night, Genie confirmed it: She would no longer be singing in the choir, something she had done all of her life and dearly loved. As difficult as it must have been for her to give it up, she did not complain or express regret. The ultimate pragmatist. She dealt with the reality at hand.

That wasn't the only love Genie would lose. Playing bridge was next. As newlyweds, we had taken bridge lessons at the YWCA in Amarillo. At first, we saw it as a way to join other lawyer couples. Several of the husbands — all husbands and no wives — had been my classmates in law school and had ended up with jobs at Amarillo law firms. The Y's bridge instructor suggested that we come to the Bridge House some weekend and learn to play duplicate bridge, which involves each competing couple playing the same arrangement of cards. Scoring is based on relative performance. Genie immediately said, "Max, let's do it. I'm having so much fun."

We played duplicate bridge with our lawyer friends and with a group from our church. Genie volunteered for us to be the custodians of the bridge boards with the responsibility to have them sorted before each session. As always, Gene Alice wanted to be in charge, especially when it was something she loved.

Duplicate bridge with the church group was invigorating at first. But as Genie's memory worsened, she grew increasingly unhappy with the game. She was having to think harder and was doubting that she had made the right bid or played the right card. On the way home one night, she said, "Max, I think we should let Sherry know that we will not be able to be regular members of the club. I find it too frustrating to play. I used to enjoy it so much."

I wondered what would be next. Her world was shrinking, and I was powerless to stop it. At least for now, she was following the recommendation to exercise with gusto. In addition to joining me on my morning jog, she immediately signed up to join five longtime friends for a Monday morning Pilates class. A photo of six fit, beautiful women was, and perhaps still is, on prominent display at the Austin Pilates Center.

Gene Alice planned to drive herself to class, but after twice taking a wrong turn from which she was able to immediately correct her errors, she apparently had had enough. "Max, why don't you drive me to Pilates and take Olive for a long walk while we have our session with Wendy?" It was her clever way of solving a memory problem. This was our pattern for the next several years. Max the chauffeur and dog walker. Genie the passenger and Pilates student.

She also continued jogging with me, but not many weeks after starting her Pilates class, she said, "Max, I don't really enjoy jogging. I know it means a lot to you, and you have to slow down to stay with me. Why don't you do the jogging, and I will do the Pilates?"

Gene Alice prized independence, and not just for herself. She didn't want to hold anyone back, and I realized she had been getting stressed running with me. As her memory loss progressed, I noticed a pattern: She would stop taking part in an activity, even ones she loved, when her independence or someone else's was thwarted. She made the decision herself and didn't wait for someone else to intervene and suggest it. Perhaps, in some strange way, that still left her feeling in control somehow. She was losing control of a skill but by acting on that knowledge, she was seizing back control of her life. I saw this play out many times.

On one of our Baltic cruises, we had a half-day stopover in Visby, Sweden. Genie and I elected to stay on the ship and read, but as she looked out of the window at the quaint city sparkling beside the water, she had second thoughts. "Max, I'm going to stroll into town and do a little window shopping," she said. I offered to go with her, but she insisted that it was just a short distance and she would enjoy strolling by herself. I watched from our cabin window as she turned into the streets leading to the center of town. When she returned, she told me that she went into several shops and was "having a ball" seeing wonderful new fabrics and local paintings. I was surprised when she said, "I wasn't going to tell you, but when I left the last shop, I could not remember which way to go to get back to the boat. Fortunately, the saleslady in the shop was watching me. She knew I was from one of the ships. She took me by the arm and led me down to the street that goes directly to the port. She gave me a hug and said, 'Darling, your ship is right down there.' I don't think I will do that again."

Driving was next. When we returned from church one Sunday, Genie's leased Park Avenue Buick was not in the carport. Tire tracks in our neighbor's yard indicated it had been towed away. We reported it to the police. One week later, the investigating detective called to tell me, "Mr. Sherman, I have good news and have bad news. The good news is that we have located your car. The bad news is that it was totaled after the thief ran it into a concrete bunker."

Genie and I located the salvage yard where the Buick had been towed, recovered as many items from the trunk as possible, and started to drive home. Even though Genie had nothing to do with that unfortunate turn of events, she saw an opportunity and took control. "Max, I think this is an omen that we should just have one car," she said. "Let's not replace it. You can drive me to some of my activities or I can get a lift from one of my friends." This is something that Genie would have never said. We were from a generation that equated having a car with freedom and independence. Her statement meant one thing: She was genuinely frightened that, if she continued to drive, she might hurt someone. From that moment on she was free of that worry, and it never loomed as a threat to her independence. I was happy to take her anywhere she wanted to go. So were her friends. She never took the wheel again.

Chapter Forty-one

Our house on Greenway Street in Central Austin was Gene Alice's dream home. Her architect brother had designed it. It was not "a show-off house." It was a house where every room had a purpose. Every wall was a gallery for works of art. Every corridor had a window to the outside. I worried that our plan to give it up and move to a life-care retirement community would be too difficult and too emotional for her to ultimately carry out. How wrong I was!

Our new community, a place where retirees could live independently and segue, as needed, to assisted living, skilled nursing, and even memory care, relieved her of the concern that I would be the one to take care of her if her memory kept failing. It also was an insurance policy to protect me from worrying about what would happen to her if I died or became incapacitated. I had already become her secretary, chief cook, and bottle washer. Each week I filled the pill boxes. I kept the calendar to remind us of all of our appointments and daily activities. I was the one who said, "It's time to go," when we had fifteen minutes to get wherever. I put out the cereal and fruit for breakfast and reminded her when it was time to go to the dining room for another meal. I realized that I was now taking care of all of the "invisible tasks" that Gene Alice had quietly assumed responsibility for in all our years of marriage.

She had contributed far more than half to our Partnership, and I hadn't really noticed. Until now.

I tried to be careful when I reminded her that we should start getting dressed for church, or a musical event, or just to meet friends for dinner. I knew that she would resent my telling her what to do. I was not the boss.

She was in heaven at our meetings with the marketing department at Westminster Manor. She picked out countertops, wood for cabinets, locations of ceiling fans, and walls that would need to be eliminated to make room for her grand piano. She enthusiastically chose paint colors, especially for her signature statement: the accent wall. Wherever we had lived, we always had at least one accent wall, and preferably, two. From our very first upstairs rental apartment to our first little house, with an orange accent wall in the dining room and a blue one on the front porch, we kept the theme going.

At Westminster, Genie chose two dark rose-colored walls, one to the left as you entered the apartment, as a backdrop for the dining table, and the other to the far right, as a way to highlight her beloved piano. She explained to Westminster's sales rep that those two walls also would be beautiful for The Happening, the abstract painting our family created in the backyard of our little house in Amarillo and a Malou Flato painting of Cuernavaca that Genie and the children had given me one year for Father's Day.

Gene Alice was an art gallery docent as she walked through our Greenway house with the architectural consultant to put Post-it Notes on paintings to take to our new home. When the apartment was ready, the consultant brought her assistant to hang the paintings, something Genie had always done herself. This time, she simply sat back nodding her head to approve of the location; the paintings would be just where she wanted them.

Chapter Forty-two

By February 2012, we had cleared the last two hurdles on the way to move into Westminster Manor. Angela gave me a list of the twelve boxes that now commemorated our lives, all indexed, labeled, and stacked in the attic. For Genie's seventy-fourth birthday she got the gift she most wanted: peace of mind. It came in form of a letter from Westminster, saying we could move into our new apartment. The redo was done, the pictures hung, even some furniture was arranged. "Max, let's go see it!" Genie said, after reading the missive. We made a hurried visit, and she was quite pleased. It was more than an antidote to her anxiety. It was her art gallery, and it met all of her aesthetic requirements. We alerted the troops, including the movers and our children, that we needed them to help us move in on April 12.

Nine years after Genie's first evaluation at the Center for BrainHealth and two-and-a-half years after we put our names on the priority list at Westminster, we moved into a new third-floor apartment. Off the living room, Genie and I stood at the rail of our large balcony overlooking seventy-eight acres of green space. She reached over to give me a hug and a kiss. "We're going to love living here," she said.

And live we did.

We continued to travel, spending several weeks each summer in Montana and sometimes going abroad, including cruising on a 200-passenger ship from Santiago to Buenos Aires. In Austin, we took the Westminster bus full of music-loving residents to almost every event featuring the opera or symphony. We would sit in our reserved seats to the left-front side of the parterre where Genie could watch the hands of the pianist.

We established new routines. Each morning, we took our newspaper out to the commons area where we would sit in wonderful wooden rocking chairs and read and discuss current events. We went weekly to Westminster's art class where Genie produced creative watercolors. We walked Olive three or four times a day around the manicured grounds and nearby neighborhood streets. In the afternoons, we shared the chaise lounge on the balcony with Olive lying at our feet. We rarely missed a Sunday morning worship service at University Presbyterian Church.

Although Genie's memory continued to fade, she was still herself. She relied on me more but continued to dote on me. When she thought my hair was getting too long, she would take a pair of scissors, a brush, and a comb to give me a trim, just as she had done countless times throughout our marriage. She had not stopped playing the piano, and she returned to an old love: the organ.

On Wednesday afternoons, I was the chauffeur who took her to our church for organ practice with Scott, her teacher. I carried the music and her laced-together organ shoes in a satchel, something she would never have let me do over the many years I went with her to hear her practice. Had I attempted to pick them up and carry them into the church she would have rebuked me. "Those are mine, Max, not yours."

As we sat in the choir loft awaiting Scott's arrival, she carefully put on those sad-looking, well-worn shoes that had been her constant companion for most of our married life. For a long while in Austin, though, when we were both busily working at the University of Texas, the shoes were relegated to the back of Gene Alice's closet. But in Amarillo, they got a good workout each week: She practiced on Saturdays and played the organ for two Sunday morning services, one at 8:30 and the other at 11:00. It took a big bite out of our free time together. When we moved to Austin, she reached over to give me one of those telltale hugs saying, "Max, it's time for us to have the freedom to use our weekends as we choose. No more organ."

Clearly, she had missed it. Now, her hour-long sessions with Scott were not for the church or for me. Whether intentionally or intuitively, it was her way to keep her mind active without committing herself to many weekend hours. Best of all, it involved something she loved.

Perhaps Genie could still play the piano and organ because the part of the brain where musical memory resides is different than the part Alzheimer's attacks. In other areas of her life, though, the disease continued its cruel march. It was taking away more and more pieces that added up to Gene Alice. Although we continued to spend time on our hand-held Nintendo games, Genie gradually quit challenging me to "move up to the next level." She was content to keep playing the easier versions.

In Montana, she no longer said, "Max, let's go fishing." For many Montana summers, we would wade separately along different streams of the river. As she began to feel uncomfortable on a stream with no one in sight, she told me about her worry. "Max, we are getting older and it is probably not safe for us to be wading in fast water. Let's get a guide so that we can be in the same boat and continue to fish all along the Yellowstone. A guide will choose the best stretch for the day, bring our lunch, and help us catch fish." That was our pattern for the last few summers.

At the symphony and the orchestra, she twice headed off to the restroom at the intermission and forgot how to get back to her seat. Fortunately, there were always friends around to guide her. I didn't realize there had been a problem until she started asking me to walk her to the restroom during the performance, something she would never have done in the past. Gradually, it struck me that we would eventually quit going to the symphony and the opera.

She loved creating multi-colored paintings, but those also became too much of a challenge. She moved from painting an elephant wearing an orange turban with a splotch of blue waves at the bottom and the notation, "He has to have somewhere to pee," signed *Gene S*, to much less intricate work involving little color, no caption, and no signature.

She still walked with me in Westminster's commons area, but she no longer wanted to sit to read and discuss the morning newspaper. She also balked at cutting my hair when I suggested, "Genie, do you think I need a trim?"

I mourned each of these losses like a survivor watching old friends pass away. Who, or more precisely, what would be next to go? As Genie's partner and caretaker, I was the keeper of this sad list. Playing the organ was the exception. She never tired of going to the church to play with Scott as long as I made all of the arrangements.

Chapter Forty-three

Whne we saw Dr. Hart for Genie's December 2013 session, I told him about this series of losses and several other memory glitches. My list did not seem to worry him. "Almost all of these are symptomatic of dementia," he said. "There may come a time when something earth-shattering occurs, but she still has impeccable appearance and superb self-confidence. Rarely do I see a patient work the room with handshakes and with her eyes as she does. That is why I asked her to bring her journal for today's session."

He rolled his wheelchair, which he had been in since our first meeting, across from Gene Alice, looked her in the eye, and said, "Gene, why don't you tell me of some of the fun memories you have written about in your journal. I don't want to hear about family, children, or grandchildren, but three or four fun times that you would consider outside the box."

As she flipped through her journal she said, "This may come as a surprise to Max, but my most favorite memory is coming out of the water at Lizard Island, standing on the sand and feeling the water drip off of my body."

"Tell me more about it," Dr. Hart said.

"I loved snorkeling at Lizard Island, snow skiing in Montana, Colorado, and New Mexico, and catching big fat trout. Activities that are part of my life because Max loved me and challenged me to give it a try."

She went on: "I had to add Lizard Island because it challenged me to reach out into the stratosphere way beyond my comfort zone. I was always afraid of water. I could paddle, but I did not really know how to swim. When the tide went out as we relaxed in our cabana at that northernmost island of Australia, Max coaxed me to swim with him. I agreed, as long as he would hold my hand. Holding hands, we swam among underwater coral valleys and mountains. We swam side by side with the most beautiful psychedelic life below the surface. We swam from coral valley to coral valley for well over an hour. It was exhilarating to step out of the water on that sandy beach. I had been to heaven."

Dr. Hart was also teaching three interns who were observing and making notes of his interview. He took Genie's hand and said, "Flip through your journal and tell me what was the most fun about being in politics."

Genie did not miss a beat. "I loved campaigning and winning, but what I loved most was walking parade routes, hurriedly shaking hands, and putting a piece of hard candy into a child's hand. I walked one side of the street and Max the other. I always wore a suit and pumps. Each of us wore a seven-inch orange badge; mine had 'Gene Alice' in bold black print. Max had only 'Max.' It was our signature for the campaign, a touch we copied from a campaign in New York City reported on in *New York Magazine*. Max and I had subscribed from the very first issue and loved to read articles and discuss them."

Dr. Hart was watching every movement in her face and the occasional use of her hands to make a point. "Think of two or three special high-level events and then tell me about one of them," he said.

"Here is one about the time we violated all rules by shaking the hand of the Queen of England," Genie said, flipping through her journal. "Here is one about the time Max and I were invited by the mother superior of a group of Carmelite nuns to take communion from Pope John Paul in San Antonio. This one is about dinner with the royal family of Nepal, but here is my favorite, walking with Georgia O'Keeffe in her garden."

"Gene, why is that so important?"

"I love art and beautiful things."

The garden walk with the famous artist was in 1977. I was the new president of West Texas State University, and Genie and I had become friends with Ted and Ruby Reid, graduates and loyal supporters of the school. Ted invited us to join them for a visit with Georgia O'Keeffe, who had been one of his teachers at West Texas Normal College. Several publications reported that he and O'Keeffe had been lovers and that he once held a cache of her paintings that his granddaughter later sold.

"I will never forget walking through Georgia's garden at her home in Abiquiu as she held Max's arm to steady herself on the cobblestones, listening to her describe how she and her sister Catherine put in the garden and chose the flowers and plants," Genie told Dr. Hart. "I think I remember it in such detail because Max later told me that Georgia, as she asked us to call her, leaned over to him and asked, 'That was what I just described, wasn't it? All I see now are shadows, so I have to do it from memory.' Even through the shadows, she saw beauty."

Dr. Hart gathered his students around him. "I have never had another patient who could do that," he said, as Genie, Holly, and I listened.

Then, addressing me and Holly, he added: "She should be

much worse, but she isn't. If you do not see some change this year, there is no need for her to see me next year."

She continued to surprise us by doing things she enjoyed. We canceled the December 2014 appointment, which made it possible to make plans to take the family to South Carolina for Christmas that year. I thought we were climbing Kilimanjaro, reaching the peak of a mountain we never thought we could climb.

Chapter Forty-four

The yin and yang of Alzheimer's is vividly demonstrated by two events in 2014: our last summer in Montana and Christmas with the family at the Isle of Palms, South Carolina.

Since the late 1980s, Gene Alice and I summered at our place in Livingston, Montana. Soon after we arrived for two months in 2014, I urged Genie to buy a sketchbook and do a drawing each day. She liked the idea and put together an accomplished book of fifteen sketches. Three of my favorites are her self-portrait, which she dated June 24, 2017, even though she was off by three years, and two of me for which I dutifully modeled. One was the real me, an old codger with glasses and a beard; the other was of a young guy in a mock turtleneck that she labeled, "You look so very young." The last word was underlined.

One morning we were sitting in our living room, looking out a wall of windows at the Yellowstone River. It flowed by at full bank with the Absaroka Range silhouetted against a pale blue sky with a few wisps of white clouds. A bald eagle flew by. We rushed to the deck to see it dive into the river to catch a fish. Over the years, we had seen this happen many times. On rare occasions, the fish catcher was a golden eagle. Other times, Genie would be delighted to spot a gaggle of geese or a mother duck floating by, a dozen ducklings following in single file. For three summers, we saw a family of otters that scampered from a beaver dam across the river. They would leave the river's southern bank and swim upriver to a high bank where they would cavort and slide, over and over, down the waterfall that cascaded into the river.

Throughout our married life, one of my joys was watching Genie enjoy the natural world. Although she grew up in the bleak, rugged hills of the Canadian River Breaks in the northern Texas Panhandle, she was captivated by scenic landscapes. Even in the Panhandle, she delighted in spring foliage tours to see blooming cottonwood trees along the few streams. Her mother once took Genie and her brother, Carl, to the northern New Mexico mountains to see actual running snow-fed streams and forests. Tavia painted those scenes in the happy days of her marriage to Bernard. Genie chose two of them to hang in our new Westminster apartment.

At our first little house in Amarillo, Gene Alice planted a small flower garden in our pitiful backyard and put a wire fence around it to keep out Jeff, our basset hound. One of my favorite memories is when Jeff violated protocol and started sniffing around in the garden. She discovered the intruder and, in floppy sandals, rushed out of our small kitchen, yanked that sixty-pound dog by the collar, and admonished him. "Don't you ever do that again!" Jeff got the message and never got close to her garden. He did not want to land back on her furious list.

Several times on our various ski trips to Montana, she would ski off the manicured slopes on trails of her making, a few yards into the trees with unbroken powdered snow. I worried that she would fall or break a leg. She loved seeing the snow-laden trees and feeling the fresh powder kicked up into her face. When I thought we would have to go find her, her shrill, very loud whistle reverberated from the trees as her all-red ski outfit popped out of a slot in the trees. She was always laughing and smiling. She was in another of her heavens.

As she watched the bald eagle that morning, Genie suddenly let go of the delightful image and turned to me. "Where did I meet you?" she asked. I was taken aback and went on automatic pilot. I started to relate the jailhouse story. She was not interested.

"When did I meet you?" she asked. I redirected her gaze to an osprey that was diving for a trout. She was back with me and grabbed my arm. "Oh, Max, isn't it wonderful!" she said.

Her mood had changed so abruptly from happy to serious to happy again. I almost put it out of my mind but should have reported it to Dr. Hart. When he recommended canceling what would have been her December 2014 appointment, he warned us that the unexpected might occur. Had I reported Genie's unusual behavior that morning, he probably would have insisted on seeing her.

One evening, we decided to grab a burger at a restaurant in Livingston. The Sport was one of our favorite places and had endured for twenty-five summers. As we sat at a table for two looking at the photos of newspaper front pages hanging on the wall nearby, my beautiful wife of fifty-three years smiled and looked intently at me across the table, "When did I meet you?"

"Oh, you know, I fell in love with you the first times I laid eyes on you," I said in the calmest voice I could muster. She smiled and picked up her hamburger. Was she forgetting who I was? Was she forgetting about *us*?

Six months later, we were at the Isle of Palms in an unbelievably beautiful HomeAway vacation rental. It was just outside of Charleston and overlooked the Atlantic Ocean. Spending Christmas in this spacious, well-appointed home with our children and granddaughters was our gift to them.

In a holiday greeting to family and friends the following Christmas, we included three photos from those days that capture how special it was for all of us. Two photos show us on the street in front of a restaurant in Charleston. In one, Gene Alice is hugging me from the back and smiling; in the other, she poses with Holly and all six grandgirls. The third photo is from Christmas morning where the six grands stand three to her left and three to her right, all dressed in identical black and white checked pajamas. Genie is quite the fashion plate, posing in a red turtleneck sweater and black slacks.

It wasn't all fun for Genie, though. I hadn't realized how unsettling it can be for someone with Alzheimer's or dementia, for that matter, to change routine and environment, all at once.

Our clan of ten had arrived at our holiday home about one o'clock in the morning. Genie and I were exhausted. The kids insisted that we take the top floor master bedroom suite. It was lovely and larger than our first 800-square-foot home in Amarillo. It also had remote-controlled blackout curtains, which we closed. There was not a ray of light in the room. When I awoke the next morning, I was aware that Genie had made a trip to the bathroom and had returned to bed. After a few minutes, I turned over to see her lying fully awake staring at the ceiling. When I reached over to give her a kiss, she said, "This place is spooky. When do we leave?" I reassured her that it was our bedroom for the week and that we were there to be with our granddaughters and our children for the Christmas holidays. She reiterated: "Spooky, too much space."

I knew by then that Gene Alice's abrupt statements and questions were often warning signs of anxieties she could not suppress. As we were getting dressed, I put my hand on her shoulder to again reassure her. She snapped back, "Don't mess with Genie while she is under stress!" I had to laugh. She always knew exactly how she felt.

Chapter Forty-five

Gene Alice and I were on a journey marked by uncertainty. I realized projecting too much into the future could be anxiety-producing and would hinder my desire to live in the moment, which is so important when a loved one has Alzheimer's. I thought back to 2005, when Gene Alice had her first two-year revisit to the Center for BrainHealth. She was doing very well, but I was afraid that we were sitting on a ticking bomb. What if "nothing to worry about" morphed into advanced Alzheimer's? What if Genie could not enjoy the music she loved? I imagined that a life without music for Gene Alice Wienbroer Sherman would be hell. I talked to our kids and several friends about my worries. We all agreed it was important to do something to honor Genie's love of music: I would pledge to finance a chair in sacred music at Austin Presbyterian Theological Seminary in Gene Alice's name. Word of my pledge made our local newspaper, *The Austin American-Statesman*, on June 12, 2005. It included a few quotes from me and the story of our chance meeting at the Hutchinson County Jail decades ago.

"Our roots go back to music and public service," I told the paper. "I've always gotten most of the recognition, but everything I've done has been in partnership with her. In many ways, she's made it possible for me to be recognized."

It took a decade to complete the pledge, which included not only the sacred music chair but the final build-out of University Presbyterian Church's majestic pipe organ. A Fort Worth church organ builder, Dan Garland, would add new pipes and complete the project. In a letter to Ted Wardlaw, president of the seminary, almost one year after Dr. Hart told us we could cancel the 2014 appointment if there were no significant changes, I wrote to Wardlaw, acknowledging my final payment on the pledge:

"Dan Garland, whose mother suffered from dementia over the last years of her life, loved GA. They became very close after she picked him to build the organ. He is doing a 162-rank organ in Ft. Worth but is making a special effort to finish UPC's before Easter. All of this in honor of GA."

Gene Alice's work on the sanctuary renovation and acquiring the original organ went back to 1995. Because of her musical background, church leaders asked her to chair a committee charged with investigating repairs to the Wicks organ that had been in the church for over fifty years. It soon became apparent that the old organ was beyond repair, so, under Gene Alice's leadership, the search for its replacement began. She did a masterful job. Everyone who knew her expected nothing less than excellence. Throughout her life, she had been a leader of organizations who excelled at making things happen. She was never pushy or prone to snapping out orders. She was more like Leonard Bernstein, an orchestra conductor who elicited responses that benefited the entire philharmonic.

People loved her. She was a patient listener and always was interested in hearing the views of others. But she also had a no-nonsense, take-charge demeanor when it came to accomplishing a task. Once she had gathered the evidence, she was ready to move to a decision. "If you know what to do, just do it," she would say.

The Church Organ Committee soon expanded into a Sanctuary Renewal Committee, with Gene Alice in charge. Our pastor remarked on her "gentle but firm leadership," and gushed that she had been "masterful' at chairing the committees. Not only did Genie oversee the acquisition of new pipe organ, she steered major changes to the sanctuary, including adding two layers of hard wall to the ceiling to reduce noise and improve the acoustics. It would enhance all forms of worship in music. The committee also called for removing numerous seats, which churches never do, to allow more room for congregants to move in and out of the pews and to angle pews so that the congregation was more intimately a part of the worship service, not just spectators.

The church's organ dedication fell on the weekend of Gene Alice's seventy-seventh birthday, February 7, 2015, twelve years after her first evaluation at the BrainHealth center. To celebrate her birthday and the organ's completion, we invited to dinner seventeen music lovers, including our church organist, our choir director, our pastor, and Peter Richard Conte, player of the world's largest pipe organ, the Wanamaker, in the Grand Court at Macy's in Philadelphia. Conte would play at the church dedication ceremony the next day. We dined at one of Genie's favorites, Tarry House. She did not engage in the conversation, but, just as if she were talking to Dr. Hart, she smiled and looked every speaker in the eye. It was beautiful.

At 3 p.m. the next day, the organ was dedicated before a congregation packed with family, new friends from Westminster, and old friends. Gene Alice relished so many coming by to give her a hug. If she were in heaven, so was I. That evening, we had another dinner at Tarry House for family and lifelong friends. Once again, she listened, smiled, and hugged. She was the young woman I married, living life to its fullest as she was able. I thanked God for that weekend.

But given the yin and yang of Alzheimer's, heaven can abruptly change to hell. Experts describe the affected individual's descent like falling off a cliff. I can testify that it feels the same to the caregiver. We had drifted from MCI to mild Alzheimer's, and now it felt like we were sinking deeper into Alzheimer's.

In the week after the organ dedication activities, I started noticing changes that Dr. Hart had warned us about. They involved our daily ritual. At breakfast, for example, Genie had been letting me put out the cereal, banana, and blueberries but would still come into the kitchen asking, "How can I help?" In the days following her organ high, she no longer came into the kitchen. After setting the table, I had to call to her and announce that breakfast was ready. It was as if she had forgotten that breakfast was something you do after waking up. Another thing: She stopped asking me if I thought it was a good time to take Olive for a walk. It never occurred to me that she probably was concerned that she would not find her way back to our apartment if she walked Olive. But now she wasn't thinking about *anyone* walking our dog.

Olive had been diagnosed with bladder cancer, and she would have accidents on the floor. Gene Alice had always been the one to rush over, clean up the errant poop, and flush it down the commode. But soon after her time in organ heaven, she no longer picked up after Olive. She would simply sit in her chair watching daytime TV shows, something she had once deemed a complete waste of time. She still showed affection to Olive, and neither one of us could bring ourselves to say we needed to think seriously about putting her down. But Olive's increased accidents and lethargy convinced me that the time had come. Through a friend, I hired a wonderful vet named Maggie who came to our apartment to euthanize our beloved companion. Maggie was a gift from God. Genie held Olive in her arms as she died from the drug. We cried, and Maggie offered to take Olive's body to a pet cemetery. That was another blessing.

As I wondered if the grief of Olive's death had accelerated Gene Alice's descent, more unhappy surprises were coming.

Chapter Forty-six

The volcano that simmered deep within Gene Alice's mind erupted one morning in, of all places, the elevator at Westminster. We were heading out to her weekly Pilates session to join her five friends. I made the breakfast, laid out her workout clothes, and nudged her: "Let's be on time." I held her hand as we hurried to the elevator. She was smiling. "Oh, don't worry," she said. "They won't start without me."

As the elevator reached the garage floor where our VW was parked, she backed away to the far side of the elevator, crouched with her shoulders hunched back, looked me straight in the eyes, and exploded. "I'm not going to that place again!" I am certain she did not know what "that place" was, just as she had no idea where or what "the club" or "the school" were. Her powerfully ingrained instinct was for her to decide whether to go or not go somewhere. I was out of line to think I was in charge. She had always jealously guarded her right to be in charge of decisions affecting her; that was the key to her identity. I had failed to appreciate that fact on that morning, alone in the elevator with Genie. I now realize that, to her, I was a drill sergeant incessantly barking orders: "Get in line. You are out of step. Hurry up, you're late." Do this. Do that. It wasn't just about leaving the house and being on time for appointments. I was making all of the decisions:

I chose the TV shows to watch.

I chose the food we ate.

I chose the clothes she wore.

I did the driving.

I read the map and determined the route, something she had always done.

I selected the paragraph from the newspaper for us to read together and then read it to her.

I suggested it was time to take the dog for a walk.

I urged her to play the piano.

And my ultimate insult was to say, "Let's be on time."

Inside her, the Genie I had always known was shouting, "I am Genie! Don't treat me like a thing. I am Genie. I am a strong, confident woman."

I was stealing Genie from Genie, nibble by nibble. In the midst of the storm, I forgot that I was her partner, not her parent. Instead of making every decision for her, I should have asked what she wanted:

Would you prefer chocolate or strawberry ice cream?

What do you want to watch tonight, a comedy or a spy story?

Should we sing hymns or songs from musicals?

Are you about ready to go to bed?

Most of the time she would say, "Oh, you decide." But I had missed the headline. She wanted to be asked. No, she needed to be asked. She wanted to be treated like she was someone, like Genie. And now she had to defend herself or risk totally losing her autonomy. All of this is obvious to me now, but in the moment, I was furious. I exploded with my own profusion of pent-up frustration that morning. "Don't ever say that again. We are going to keep exercising, working puzzles, reading books, seeing movies, doing everything possible to stay alive as long as we are alive."

I didn't realize it then, but I was grieving, just as all caregivers mourn the lives they once had and the persons their loved ones had been before Alzheimer's marked them indelibly. I wanted my Genie back.

Chapter Forty-seven

The next wave of the Alzheimer's tsunami came at three o'clock in the morning. I was sound asleep and snoring, I'm sure. I was awakened by a persistent knocking on the apartment door. When I opened it, the night security grade was standing there, holding Gene Alice's hand. She had silently slipped out of our bed to go somewhere she desperately needed to be. It was not a place she could name to either of us. The security guard noticed her at the secured exit to our complex. She was confused and disoriented. She did not know who she was or why she was there. She could not answer his gentle questions, "May I help you? Would you like to return to your apartment? What is your name?"

She appeared distraught. The guard put his arm around her, hugged her, and waited for her to relax. Calmly, she told him her name and her apartment number. He took her by the hand and led her back. She was so happy to see me. She gave me a big hug, took my hand insisting, "Let's go to bed." We snuggled and drifted off to sleep.

The little waves kept coming in middle-of-the-night departures and returns. Then, she started leaving in the afternoon. The evidence was hauntingly clear. She had moved into a far more serious, and potentially dangerous stage of Alzheimer's. As required by law, her wanderings were written up and reported to the head nurse, Dianne. She was concerned about Genie's safety and made an appointment with me to decide a course of action. "What do we do with Ms. Sherman?" she asked. "Is it time for her to go to memory care? If she stays here, how do we keep her from wandering? Do you think you can handle it?"

To me, memory care was a nursing home. As a young lawyer, I often went with clients to nursing homes to get legal papers signed. The halls were always lined with wheelchairs occupied by catatonic people I had known throughout my life and who now were shells of their former selves. When they were still cognizant of their surroundings, I heard them plead to their loved ones. "Don't put me away. Please, don't put me away."

After Dr. Hart diagnosed Genie's dementia as Alzheimer's in 2007, I told our kids, "It scares the hell out of me! I don't think I can put her in the memory unit. I can take care of her." When Gene Alice and I agreed to move into a retirement community as an insurance policy to protect her in the event I died or became incapacitated, it never occurred to me that I would someday have to make the decision for us to live apart and for her to be in memory care. That was not something I ever wanted, and I made my feelings known to the nurse.

Dianne understood. She recommended installing a nighttime brake on our door, as others had done to keep a loved one from wandering. But I knew that Genie would be infuriated if she attempted to open a door and it would not budge. Our solution was to place three chairs in a triangle against the door. I assured Dianne that I would wake up if Genie started moving the chairs on the hardwood floor. It was our solution to Gene Alice's wanderings. But that plan fell apart quickly. A tidal wave was heading straight for Genie and me. It would change everything. We were sitting in the recliners that Genie had chosen several years earlier, sipping wine and watching TV. She was smiling. And then she wasn't.

"Who are you?" she said raising her voice and springing out of her chair. "What are you doing in my house? You have to get out of here!" As she rushed to the apartment door, she changed her mind and said, "I have to go. I have to go to my family. I have to go meet the girls." Then it was back to me being forced to leave. It made no sense, but I understood, without question, that she desperately wanted to get away from me. Suddenly, I was a stranger. And a threat.

That's when she tried to rush out, and we tussled at the door. I felt weak, almost faint, either from fear or my eighty years of age. She was winning the battle, and the door was starting to open. In desperation, I looked into her face and pleaded, "Let's call our son, let's call our daughter." This enraged her even more. "How dare you talk to me like that," she shouted. "I do not trust you. I do not trust you. You are not my husband."

Exhausted, I finally said something that made sense to her. "Let's call your friend Joanne and wish her a happy eightieth birthday." Joanne was one of her closest friends. It connected. She immediately said, "Joanne. Joanne. Yes. Let's call her."

Joanne has a doctorate in psychology and has interviewed hundreds of people struggling with dementia and Alzheimer's. She sensed our crisis. She kept Genie on the phone with pleasant memories from their many times together. I could hear Gene Alice laughing. A potential disaster was averted. We put the chairs in front of the door and went to bed.

A few nights later, our children, Lynn and Holly, came over to spend the evening with us. I briefed them on the tidal wave we had just experienced. Lynn took one of her hands, Holly the other. They looked into her eyes with love. She knew them, and we thoroughly enjoyed our time together. But they were hardly out of our apartment when Genie and I rushed to place the three chairs at the door. I forgot that I was only wearing socks and slipped on the well-polished wood floor. The pain was instantaneous and excruciating. I couldn't get up. Fortunately, my cell phone fell within reach. I called security and our kids, alerting them to come back right away; we needed help. Security notified the on-call nurse who arrived about the same time as the kids. She immediately recognized a very bad break. My left femur had shattered. The paramedics arrived to load me onto a gurney and whisk me off to the hospital for emergency surgery and two weeks of rehabilitation.

In the convoluted world of Alzheimer's, the waves of forgetting, not knowing, and wandering had become the tsunami that I had feared. Fortunately, we had discussed our reasons for moving to a senior living community with Lynn and Holly. Because Genie could not stay in our apartment alone, they made the decision for her to start migrating to skilled nursing and, ultimately, memory care on the campus where we lived. Out of four caregivers recommended by the head nurse, our kids chose Monique to be Genie's companion. These were all decisions I had not been prepared to make. In fact, I wonder if I could have. I always believed Genie and I could fix whatever went wrong. The Partnership would work it out. We would struggle with Alzheimer's, but we would be together. As I lay in my hospital bed, I cried, not just from grief but from guilt. "Had I failed the Partnership? Was I putting my beloved away?" It did not seem possible that the two of us who had met as kids and spent our lives together had come to this. We had promised, "Until death do us part." The next wave brought despair.

ACT IV

Chapter Forty-eight

It was pure hell returning from the hospital to an empty apartment in late March 2015. Home offered no warmth, no love. Genie was gone. What I would have given to hug, kiss, or kid around with her. My sun-soaked world had turned dark and cold. The Alzheimer's tsunami had swallowed our lives. I wallowed in my sadness those first few days and wondered how people find the strength to go on in the midst of heartbreak and loss. I didn't have to guess for long.

Memories of my early days as a newly minted lawyer came to my rescue. I recalled how I had sat with families facing the decision of "what to do with Mom" when the doctor urged them to find a memory care unit where she could live. Those families received the same professional advice I had been given while in the hospital. "Don't go to see her for several weeks. She has to know that where she is now is her home. If you come to visit, she will never accept the move. It will be difficult for you and for her, but, in the long-run, it will make your lives much better." At the law firm, I had met with families who did not follow that advice and could not stay away from their loved one.

"How do we get Mom out of that place?" they would ask me. "She is miserable." They were miserable, too, and probably wracked by guilt. I felt all of that — and more. What had I done? I was overwhelmed by grief and doubt as I stumbled into one of the most difficult times in my life. But I knew there was a well-trod path forward, if I could just put my heartache aside. I followed the professional advice and stayed away from the person I loved most.

I was still in pain from the break and limped around the apartment like a wounded animal. The injury had been severe, and I was facing a long and tedious recovery. Still, I had no idea nine months would pass before I would visit Genie's new home or she would visit the apartment.

Thank God I found Zelda.

Chapter Forty-nine

Zelda, a ten-pound, six-year-old Shih Tzu, was my constant companion during what would have otherwise been an unbearably lonely time in what had been "our" apartment. Now it was mine and Zelda's.

I was not completely devoid of company of the two-legged variety. Almost immediately after the word was out that Genie was in the memory unit at Westminster with Alzheimer's, longtime and even casual friends started showing up to talk with me about it. The stigma of never — or at least, hesitantly — using the word "dementia" and certainly not "Alzheimer's" evaporates when a loved one is diagnosed with one or the other. In my first weeks of isolation from Genie, I was an outlet for anguished stories from friends and acquaintances who came calling. It may have been a parent, a spouse, a brother, or a sister, but friends needed to describe their journeys with Alzheimer's.

Jerry was a retired judge. His mother had died ten years earlier, after a decade-long struggle with Alzheimer's. Jerry and I had known each other since law school. We were good friends but not super-close. We had not seen each other for several months. While I was still in the hospital, Jerry called and asked if he could visit. "I would like to tell you about my mother," he said. On the first of several daily visits to the hospital, Jerry shared his pain as he reluctantly accepted the reality of his mother's disease. She began to wander in the neighborhood. His father installed a device to prevent her from opening the door, but it did not solve the problem. One day his father came in from his workshop in the backyard to find the family car packed with all of her clothes. "I have to go home," his wife of sixty-three years announced.

Jerry wept as he related a second episode. One evening he joined his parents to take Mom out for dinner. Mother, father, and son were sitting in the car ready to depart when his mother blurted out, "We can't go without Daddy!" Jerry listened as his dad said, much like I had tried to explain when I stared into the mouth of the ferocious lion, "Honey, your daddy died nearly thirty years ago." She would not hear of it; she most certainly did not want an explanation. She became more agitated and insistent. "We can't go without Daddy!" she screamed.

A light came on for Jerry. "Mom, I just talked to Daddy. He doesn't want to go now." His mother was satisfied. A fib made up on the fly solved the crisis. The family had dinner without Daddy.

My next awakening came soon after I returned to my apartment to learn a lesson I had failed to grasp as a young lawyer in training. It was the first time I spoke with Gene Alice on the phone. I knew how to give legal advice to families struggling with "what do we do with Mom," but I did not fully appreciate the daily agony they endured when hearing Mom's relentless tears and protests. "I do not belong here. You have to get me out of here." This time, I got it.

Over the next few weeks of separation from Genie, I called her every morning at ten o'clock and every evening at six o'clock. We'd talk one last time before she went to bed. Her calls to me were spontaneous, usually when she told a helper in her unit, "I need to call my husband." It was good-quality time, similar to our days of swapping tales on the phone when I was in the legislature in Austin and she was at home in Amarillo. My favorite sign-off at the end of the day was, "I'm going to send you five big love kisses to help you sleep soundly. Are you ready? Here they come. I hope they don't knock you over. Smack, smack, smack, smack, smack. Each one says love, love, love, love, love. Are you still on your feet?"

She would laugh and say, "I love you, too. Good night."

Not all of our sign-offs were so pleasant. One evening, an attendant in the memory unit alerted me via text that Genie was tired and tried to go to bed before her evening meal. I called an hour earlier than usual, and Genie answered saying, "Max, I am here in bed in my PJs." I gently but firmly told her that it was time for dinner, not for bed. Then, she pleaded. "You have to come and get me. I'm ready to come home. I am down here and ready to go. I can get my things together. I want to be with you."

I had the same yearning to see her, and if she had been any-where but there, I would have run to her. Instead, I tamped down my emotions, took a breath, and repeated an old refrain that I had been using to explain why I could not come. "I see my surgeon next week. I am still healing. When I am better, we will get together."

"Will you come to get me and take me home? How will we get together?"

I assured her that her good friend and helper, Monique, would make sure we got together very soon. As my friend Jerry had learned and taught me, a brief, direct fib can solve the crisis of the moment.

Chapter Fifty

I imagine there must be thousands, if not millions, of family members and caregivers who wonder what it must be like to be the one who has Alzheimer's. Genie and I had always shared our thoughts and experiences with each other. Often, I would imagine telling her about something that had happened to me and could hear her voice responding or laughing in my mind. It had been the same for her. After so many years together, we instinctively knew how each other would react. We had no trouble completing each other's sentences. But what was happening to her now was mysterious to me.

One night, I believe I came close to understanding Gene Alice's world, and it shook me to my core. It was one of those nights when sleep wasn't restful but cursed. Just before bed, I had rummaged through a batch of photos and had come across a group of pictures from a fun going-away party in Amarillo. We were moving from our home of twenty-two years to Austin and saying farewell to dear friends. The coup de grâce was a photo of a quilt our friends had given us. Each family created a square to depict some cherished moment from our time together as one big, happy family. Most were designed by friends from our Presbyterian church where Genie had been the organist for twenty years. Then, I realized that most of those couples were no longer intact. Each of the three couples with whom we stayed in touch had lost a spouse. Other than those three couples, all of the others who smiled at me from the photos were dead. I was sad and tired, so I went to bed.

How long does a dream or a nightmare last? A minute? Ten minutes? As long as the flash of a thought or memory or the time it takes to work through a riddle? I rarely remember my dreams and cannot recall ever having had a nightmare. But this one woke me up, leaving me terrified and sweating.

In the dream, Genie and I are at a party. All of our Amarillo friends are there, sharing laughter and stories conjured by our memories. We are all having a rollicking good time at the home of our wonderful hosts, Betsy and Don. As guests start to depart, Genie and I fold a quilt given to us by our friends and carefully place it in the back seat of our VW. I get in the driver's seat and suddenly realize I've somehow lost the ignition key. It occurs to me that I must have taken it out of my pocket when someone asked to see a photo I always carry of Genie and me on our honeymoon. The key must be inside Betsy's and Don's house. I return to their front door and notice the house is already dark. I ring the doorbell to rouse our friends, but no one answers. I tap the knocker. Still, no one. I pound on the door. Our friends are gone. But where? How could they have left in the brief moments that Genie and I had walked outside and gotten in the car? And because, back in those days, we had no cellphones or Uber to call, not having a key and a way to get home was no minor problem. My mind spins, and I'm starting to panic when the terror of it wakes me up.

Awake now, heart pounding as the dream seeps into my consciousness, I believe I've been given a glimpse inside the brain of a person with Alzheimer's. Something essential is lost, and there's no apparent way to get it back. The person is completely alone and feels helpless and abandoned. Family, friends, and caregivers are not there. She feels like screaming for help. Her body starts to shake from fear and panic. But she knows that screaming won't help; no one will hear her. She must find a phone. But she quickly realizes she doesn't even know who to call for help. She can't remember. I feel that desperation in the nightmare when I'm knocking and ringing the doorbell. I need my key, and now I realize what it's like not to have one. When something essential is lost.

Chapter Fifty-one

Residents at our retirement home continued to visit me and ask about my separation from Genie.

"What's is it like to be living apart?"

"When do you see each other?"

"Will you be able to be together again?"

They cared and wanted to know if we were OK. Some had already experienced the agony of seeing a loved one seized by Alzheimer's. Others were silently afraid that they might land in memory care someday. A woman resident and friend who was widowed and without children expressed that fear. "And I won't have someone like you to be there for me," she said.

I was realizing that the stigma surrounding Alzheimer's is not just nurtured by people who have no clue what the disease is all about. It is also alive in the memory unit.

Since our physical separation, Sundays were tough for Genie. The minutes passed slowly because activities and staff were few. Genie liked to stay busy, not get bored. She may have even become agitated when nothing was going on. Late one Sunday afternoon, early in her move to the memory unit, she was especially anxious about having nothing to do. She saw Tom, one of the two regular maintenance workers with whom we had formed a friendship, walking toward her. She motioned for him to join her and sit in the alcove at the end of the hall. Respectfully, he listened as she pointed down the hall to four women sitting in wheelchairs, a couple with heads bowed and nodding. Soon after he left, he was knocking at my door to tell me what she had said to him: "I do not want to be like them. I do not want my family to come and go to take care of me, when I do not even know they are here. I am afraid I am losing it!" She had the same assumption that most of us, including me, have — that those women in the wheelchairs have no life. The stigma of Alzheimer's is bred into us.

How wrong we are. Genie developed a reputation in the memory care unit as one who helped take care of others. On her behalf, I treasure that. I have learned so much about the four women who occupied those wheelchairs. Jane boisterously sings hymns from memory at the Sunday vespers service. Ann, who should have been a lawyer, always asks questions. Lucy makes the same request of every visitor, "Tell us a story." And then there's Marie.

One time, when Scott, the organist from our University Presbyterian Church, was invited to play hymns for a sing-along in the activity room, he asked Genie to sit by him and play some of the hymns. I brought our little Shih Tzu Zelda and pulled up a chair next to Marie. I put Zelda in my lap and started stroking her ears to keep her calm in a crowd of strangers. Marie did not raise her head or, as far as I could tell, even open her eyes. As Scott and Genie played old familiar hymns, I was suddenly spooked when a hand from nowhere began to gently stroke Zelda. It was Marie. She only appeared to be sleeping.

Brooks, who leads activities in the memory care unit, takes a group of five to eleven residents at least once, and often twice, a month to Tarrytown Methodist Church for lunch and games with senior church members. I often join them. Church members usually play dominoes and cards. The Westminster residents play Chicken Foot. Neither Gene Alice nor I had ever played this modification of a domino game. The dominoes range from nine to blank. We are a motley crew — a retired medical school professor, the widow of a minister, a high school English teacher, an organist, and many others who once had challenging careers. Different skills show up during the game. We have fun. When one of us wins, the others applaud and often shout. We are very much with it. No stigma here.

Slowly, I was learning that in the Bleak House of Alzheimer's love is fragile and often on the brink of losing its power. If one is not careful, everything can become medical, pharmaceutical, clinical, legal, agonizing, suffocating, both to the beloved with Alzheimer's and to the lover-caregiver. It pays to play.

Several times I have convinced myself not to talk about the devastation created when an Alzheimer's tsunami sweeps across your life. That would not be fair to Genie or to me. Death and doubt are real and raw. I thought Genie and I were dying, if not already the walking dead. In one of our telephone conversations she pleaded, "If you don't come and take me home, I will die down here." A part of me died when she said that.

I needed guidance to navigate the rough waters that continued to rush toward me. I had my Christian faith. I had prayed throughout my life for things big and small. This one was tough and required a lot of thinking and praying for God's help.

How do I sum up my faith, this belief that while we can't see God, we have faith and hope in God's mercy? Love. God is love. Genie and I never sat down to have this discussion; it was just understood. She from being enveloped in a Christian church all of her life. Me from being loved by my recently divorced mother and her three sisters who were my mother and father for my first eleven years. I never doubted that I was loved. I have never doubted God's love, either. It now sustains me, and I believe it sustains Gene Alice. I have no way of knowing what goes on in the mind of a person deep in the forest of Alzheimer's, but I feel confident she breathes every breath knowing that God loves her as I do. Even in moments of intense pain as her life's partner, I have never doubted God's love for both of us.

In our Christian faith, Lent is a time when we are preoccupied with death. It begins with Ash Wednesday, which, during the Alzheimer's tsunami, was Genie's bolt from the apartment shouting, "You're not my husband." Lent four years later, almost to the exact date, I am dealing with death and dying because I understand what advancing Alzheimer's can do. I'm also in my eighties and know that all life has an expiration date. To better understand death, the good student in me said, "Go to the books." And, I did. I read Stephen Jenkinson's *Die Wise: a Manifesto for Sanity and Soul,* Atul Gawande's *Being Mortal: Medicine and What Matters in the End* and my University of Texas friend Sheldon Ekland-Olson's scholarly work, *Who Lives, Who Dies, Who Decides?: Abortion, Neonatal Care, Assisted Dying, and Capital Punishment.* These and other books were helpful, but the real understanding of Alzheimer's and how to live with it came from those who were integral to our lives.

A significant part of our family income as a newly married couple came from death and dying. Genie played for many services at funeral homes. Often, she sat with the family members as they discussed the music they wanted her to play. Later in life, she had the same experience as the church organist. She knew far more about death than her lawyer-partner ever knew. Several times we had our Partnership meeting to sort out our own end-of-life plans.

After one funeral home service, she came to our upstairs garage apartment, flung herself down on our one bed and cried, "Max, it was one of the most brutal things I've ever seen. This little girl did not want to look into an open casket to see her grandmother. She ran out the back of the mortuary. Her mother chased her and dragged her back to the casket, held her over the body insisting, 'You have got to kiss grandma goodbye.' I have never heard such screaming, 'No, no, no, I don't want to remember grandma that way.'"

I lay down beside her, hugged her, and gave her a kiss as we promised each other that we would never have a casket in the church. It would be a worship service to offer thanks for God's generosity in our lives.

Another time, she accompanied a young friend having an abortion. The ultrasound showed that the fetus was grossly deformed. The young friend said, "Genie, I can't do this alone. Will you go with me?" My Genie, who treasured the dignity of life, went with her, held her hand during the procedure, and tucked her young friend into bed afterward. When she returned to our home, we lay down on our bed, hugged, cried, and agreed that, even though it had been an incredibly painful experience, she had been a minister to a friend in need.

We were together when a relative called to tell us that he had come home from work to find his wife hanging in the garage. "Genie, you are my closest relative and friend. Would you come to help me work through this?" She immediately drove to be with him. When she returned, we lay down on our bed, hugged, and struggled with, "Why, oh, why would she do that?" Genie lay back and said a little prayer. "I know she was miserable," she said, "but I could never do that. Life is too precious."

When she was seventy-six, Tavia, Genie's mother, called from her senior living home in Lubbock to tell Gene Alice she was in the hospital. "They tell me I have pancreatic cancer and that I do not have long to live. Will you come to be with me?" Genie was on the next plane out of Austin to keep a vigil at her mother's bedside.

Two days later, she held Tavia's hand as her mother said her last words. "Give my babies a kiss."

My own mother's death on March 9, 1992, was peaceful but very different. I received a call from Katrina, a close personal friend of my eighty-five-year-old mother. "Max, Eva is in the hospital. She would love to see you. There is no urgency. It is not serious. She may go home in a day or two, but she would love to see you." That same afternoon I boarded a plane and flew 500 miles to be with my mother, rented a car, and drove the fifty miles from Amarillo to Borger. I went straight to the hospital.

My mother and I had a long visit, catching up on children and grandchildren. She had just learned that she would go home the next morning and looked forward to sleeping in her own bed. I told her that I had packed a bag and would stay with her for three or four days and that I would be there in the morning to take her home. She insisted that there was no reason for me to stay over, and she didn't want me to miss work unnecessarily. "I will be fine. You must go home to be with your family." I gave her a hug and a kiss as I left her hospital room to drive back to the airport. I caught the last late-night flight back to Austin. When I arrived, Genie met me to tell me my mother had died soon after I left the hospital.

I was soon back in Borger to make funeral arrangements. I visited with the duty nurse from that last evening with my mother, and we talked. "It was the most beautiful death," the nurse said. "She was so happy to have said her goodbye to you. She was content. You had only been away twenty to thirty minutes when she called to tell me, 'I can see my sisters holding out their hands to welcome me to join them.' I have been a nurse for thirty years. It may have been the most beautiful death I have ever witnessed. Your mother smiled, closed her eyes as she held out her hands, 'I am going to go be with my sisters.' She peacefully let go of her life."

The sisters were with my mom from Arkansas to Texas, through many ups and downs. All three had died many years before. Had it not been my mother, I would have written off her comments about seeing her sisters as "spooky." But I believed the final words of my no-nonsense mother. She was not a particularly religious woman, but she was a woman of solid values and solid goodness. She died as she had lived. She accepted life with her hands open to receive what came, and she accepted death in the same way.

When I returned to my office, I told the story of my mother's passing to Kay, my chief of staff, close friend, and confidant. Kay had her own story. Her younger sister was married to a professor at the University of Kansas, had two small children, and had recently been diagnosed with an aggressive brain cancer. Kay flew back and forth to Kansas as often as she could to help keep the young family together and was by her sister's side as she lingered for several weeks and eventually died after radical brain surgery. Kay returned to Austin committed to help people make end-of-life decisions, which she described as "helping them cross over." She took hospice training and frequently went to bedsides of dying patients.

Kay assured me that my mother's dying was not unique. She had many experiences with people looking death in the face to see loved ones who had gone before. She related a moving experience of an elderly woman who was estranged from everyone in her family. She was dying, but there was no one there. She refused to die alone. Kay was the one who gave her permission to go. She died as Kay held her hand.

Death had been a familiar presence in my life since childhood. Knowing that my biological father had died when I was small and then seeing my stepfather die less than six years after my mother married him, made death an unavoidable topic. In high school, my friend Larry and I were asked to be pallbearers for Bob, a casual friend, who was killed in a car accident on a trip from Borger to Amarillo. Bob had more friends from another high school in the next town, friends who spent hours together rehearsing and acting in plays. Bob reveled in marching to a drumbeat only he could hear. He was often gloomy, but his close friends knew another side of him. Larry and I sat quietly in the pallbearer limousine during our fifty-mile trip to the cemetery. His theater friends laughed when one of them said, "Can't you just see Bob sitting on his casket reaching up to pluck stars out of the sky. He is happier than he has ever been."

The AIDS epidemic also brought death into my life — and into the lives of so many people. Before *Angels in America* came to stages in the United States, Genie put it on our London theater repertoire. We were among the first to see it at the Cotswold Playhouse. The production was raw, riveting, and brutally realistic. When the curtain rose, all 250 seats in the house were taken. After the intermission, we realized most of the audience had fled. Genie and I were among the fifty or so remaining. My guess is that the balance of the audience either had AIDS or knew someone who died from it.

Genie's New York City architect brother Carl told us about a young man in his office who had AIDS and was probably going to die from it. The young man confided in Carl that his family had disowned him and would not come to the city to be with him in his final days. He asked Carl to stand in for his family. Carl did and helped the young man die peacefully in his eighth-floor apartment. A greater horror came after his death. The New York City officials charged with dealing with the new epidemic sent workers to "cleanse" the apartment. They wore orange hazmat suits and masks and sprayed every inch of the apartment. Carl, who had been there for several days in his work clothes, was incensed. The city he loved was not prepared to deal with a kind of death it did not yet understand.

My own experience with a friend's AIDS death came about by accident. I had been appointed to fill the unexpired term of my mentor, Judge Abner McCall, on the Texas Juvenile Probation Board. I served the remainder of his term and one more. That is where I learned of the dedication of a small staff that faced super-human challenges. Malcolm was the youngest member of the board's staff. We became friends and stayed in touch after I finished my term. In my first month as dean of the LBJ School of Public Affairs, I was handed a memo informing me that one of the school's first graduates had died of AIDS. It was Malcolm. I immediately wrote a note to his partner expressing my sadness and offering my support. To my surprise, the partner asked me to be a pallbearer at Malcolm's memorial service at St. Austin Catholic Parish. I readily agreed. It was my first time in that sanctuary. Eerily, the service was much like the scene at the Cotswold Playhouse. A small crowd attended, with the stage an open casket. As I sat in the pallbearer pew, I watched young men walk past to pay their respects. As I looked around, most of them walked out the church door.

In my first month alone in my Westminster apartment, two young men, both grandchildren of friends, hanged themselves. One was almost twenty-one. The other was just one month past his twenty-first birthday. I did not know the boys, but Genie and I knew their families from years earlier. Only by chance did I see the twenty-one-year-old's newspaper obituary. He had just completed a successful freshman year at a prestigious West Coast university where he had, "quickly achieved acceptance into the National Society of Collegiate Scholars for academic excellence." He seemed to be well on his way to a highly success-ful academic career.

At the memorial service for the twenty-year-old, the printed program featured only the young man's photograph and a poem that ended with "Love doesn't die, people do. So, when all that's left of me is love, give me away."

I was reading the poem when a retired minister friend walked over. I asked him to read it with me. He was a personal friend and a fly-fishing buddy, but rather than talk about a hobby we loved, we talked about suicide.

"Am I blind or do these tragedies just happen to young men? I don't recall a suicide of any girls from friends or families we know," I said.

After forty years as a pastor, he had an informed response. "Young boys and girls are devastated when a love affair explodes. Many people struggle with sexual identity. For older people, a failing mind or lost physical ability or the death of a spouse might be the cause. I have presided at many funerals and memorial services where the deceased committed suicide, but only the family and I knew."

The stigma of suicide may be even worse than the stigma of Alzheimer's. And there's a connection between the two. The studies

show that people early in an Alzheimer's diagnosis have a significantly higher risk of dying by suicide. I struggle with the cries from
those with Alzheimer's and dementia who plead "to go home, to
join loved ones long departed." Is it a deep cry for permission to
cross over, to die? I reread a passage in a Richard Bach book Kay
gave me to help me work through my mother's death, *Illusions: The
Adventures of a Reluctant Messiah*. The passage that struck me talks
about the necessity of bidding farewell to those you love. That has
to happen before you can meet them again, Bach writes.

The partnership agreement between Genie and me about how
to handle our deaths was sound. No casket. Bodies get donated to
a medical school. Gravestones are in place with all essential infor-
mation, including "Active Presbyterian" to reinforce how important
the church was to our lives. Dying with dignity whenever that time
comes or as Austin Seminary Associate Dean Paul Hooker put it in a
poem, "Do not yet roll the stone away nor hurry toward tomorrow's
dawn. ... (T)he Possible in its unknown way will use the dark to
make us strong."

My recovery was slow and long. I spent six months going to
rehabilitation therapy sessions and appointments with my surgeon.
I used my time alone in the apartment to work my way through
stacks of paperwork that had accumulated while I was in the
hospital. Filling out forms and insurance documents was tedious
and boring. I started rummaging through some of Genie's files. I
discovered her well-marked program notes from a night in Israel
in 1976 when we heard the Israel Philharmonic Orchestra perform
Gustav Mahler's Symphony No. 2, known as the "Resurrection
Symphony," under the baton of thirty-nine-year-old Zubin Mehta.
Mahler captured the fear of death in his first movement which he
named "Funeral Rites." Mahler is quoted in the program notes as

saying, "…if you are curious, it is the hero of my First Symphony that I am burying here and whose life I am gathering up in a clear mirror, from a higher vantage point. At the same time, it is the great question: Why have you lived? Why have you suffered? Is all this merely a great, horrible jest? We must resolve these questions somehow or other, if we are to go on living — indeed, even if we are going to go on dying." The fourth movement "Urlicht" ("Primal Light") in Mahler's words, "represents the soul's striving and questioning attitude towards God and its own immortality. The moving voice of innocent belief sounds in our ears." The fifth movement is blessedly brighter and proposes renewal — the "Resurrection" promised by the title. Gene Alice had underlined resurrection in red with two exclamation marks.

So, my contemplation on how others find the strength to go on, and whether I was strong enough, led me to Mahler. He suggests that the promise of resurrection would give me the hope I needed. But the practical answer about living with Alzheimer's day in and day out came from Tavia and Eva, our strong, independent mothers, who not only brought us into this world but taught us how to leave it. Hold hands. Accept life and death. Hug. Kiss each other. Kiss the babies. Cherish one another.

Chapter Fifty-two

I missed Gene Alice terribly, but the staff did not think it a good idea for me to visit her in her room or for her to visit me in the apartment we had so recently shared together. After about four months of speaking with Genie only by phone, we met for lunch in the Bistro. I was scared about the first visit. I feared she might be angry or plead with me to take her home. Neither happened. We started meeting weekly for lunch, then more for other meals. In December 2015, nine months after returning to my lonely apartment from the hospital, I got a call from the chair of the care team at Westminster.

"Mr. Sherman," the voice said, "we think it is time for you to stop by to see Ms. Sherman. You might go down mid-morning, stay for a few minutes and be sure to have a good excuse to leave. We do not want her to think she should go with you. Don't go in the evening or close to mealtime or on Sunday, times when she has always been with you for a meal or for church. If this goes well, we will start recommending longer visits."

My first three visits to her room were strained. Genie smiled and seemed to enjoy my company, but a thought gnawed at me and opened a wound. She knew I was her Max, but I felt she acted like I was just a friend stopping by to say hello. Was she angry I was not bringing her home with me? Was she also nursing her own wound? Had I made a terrible mistake by following the advice of professionals instead of my heart? These questions tormented me when I went home alone to my apartment. I had to push them away, and the only thing I could think to do was immerse myself in the work of sorting and discarding papers and momentos that we had brought with us when we moved to Westminster. Although we had tossed a lot of old papers before the move, what we couldn't decide on faced me still. Time had been short; now I had too much.

I discovered a 2014 Christmas gift from Craig Hella Johnson, the Grammy-winning founder and artistic director of Conspirare, Austin's acclaimed choral music group. Genie was a founding director of Conspirare's board and had encouraged Craig to launch the group. His gift was a CD of the group's music. On my fourth visit to Genie's room, I took that CD. As we listened to the moving chorus of voices, Genie closed her eyes, slowly pumped her ankles as if using the pedals of the organ, and softly directed the singers, perfectly in sync with Craig. This was the beginning of our resurrection. I shared the moment with Craig in an email. He responded by sending a set of all Conspirare CDs to Genie with this note:

> *"I am so touched to know that you shared this music with Gene Alice and that it was meaningful and useful to help her connect with the music and with some peaceful part of the core of her being. Music has such a powerful and subtle way of penetrating some of our toughest human obstacles. As my father went deeper into his dementia journey, he listened over and over again to the Conspirare CDs, and I witnessed the power of human voices to comfort him, to*

bring him peace and delight. I know how much Gene Alice
has loved choral music in her life and I hope that she can
be accompanied by our music if it is something that can
bring her joy."

One day I chose the CD *Something Beautiful* and played the
last number, "I Could Have Danced All Night." As it was playing,
I stood, walked over to Genie, and said, "Shall we dance?" It was a
magical moment. We danced and then hugged. The ice had been
broken. I was not a stranger.

A few weeks later, the St. Olaf College Choir performed at
St. Martin's Lutheran Church. Eric Wall, the newly appointed
holder of the Gene Alice Sherman Chair in Sacred Music at Austin
Presbyterian Theological Seminary, attended the performance and
purchased a CD of the choir's music for Genie. Our ten-to-twenty-
minute music sessions expanded to forty-five minutes and then an
hour. She was directing, singing soprano, smiling, and thoroughly
enjoying choral music. During those hours, the old Gene Alice was
focused and content. I saw more and more the magic of shared moments, with both of us fully present.

Chapter Fifty-three

When Gene Alice moved to memory care, I was deeply afraid of the future. Would the sunny life we had shared become progressively obscured by the darkness of Alzheimer's? I feared our love story would end with a total eclipse. How wrong I was! It was becoming clear that music would be our miracle and our redemption. My iPad was my constant companion on trips to Genie's room. I would google the names of songs or performers so that we could spend an hour each morning and evening in near bliss during our visits. We would brainstorm favorite songs or performers and then sing together or dance to long-forgotten tunes.

One of the songs I often sang to Genie was "You Are My Sunshine." We were partial to Johnny Cash's version, but we added a personal touch that came to us in Montana. We were standing on the deck of our home, looking across the Yellowstone River at the Absaroka Mountains and watching the sun rise when we took the opening verse from an eighteenth century Black spiritual, modified it, and made it the song's closing lines. "My Lord, what a morning! My Lord, what a morning! Oh, my Lord, what a morning, when the sun begins to shine." Later, standing on our balcony at Westminster with Genie beside me, I started singing those joyful lines when she reached over to hug me, flashed her gorgeous smile, and joined in the singing.

Music continued to be a respite from the march of Alzheimer's. Gene Alice took great pleasure in conducting the Tabernacle Choir (formerly, the Mormon Tabernacle Choir) in time with the director who was leading 360 voices of men in formal wear and women in light blue. The choir stood in an open field singing "A Mighty Fortress Is Our God." When I play the Celtic Woman singing on my iPad, she pulls it close and intently joins in whatever song they are singing. She is one of them. A friend who brings her therapy dog, Toby, to Genie's room every two weeks emailed me, describing the joy Genie expressed when hearing Handel's "Harmonious Blacksmith."

"Gene Alice pets Toby with one hand and conducts with the other," the friend said.

I googled a rousing organ rendition of that song and witnessed her complete immersion in the music. Had there been an organ in the room Genie would have joined in a duet. She vigorously urged the Italian organist on as if the music depended on her orchestration.

One Friday night, we were in her room when we got the idea to put on Tommy Dorsey and His Orchestra. We had loved swing dancing together when we were younger, and we seamlessly danced together all evening until we were exhausted. The next morning, our living community was holding a celebration in the large common area at Westminster, which we called the commons. I spent the day running errands and was looking forward to a quiet evening. But a last-minute impulse, like a voice in my ear, insisted: "Go on down." I first dined alone in the Bistro; then I moved to the commons. Many tables were already full of residents. It was one of the most perfect evenings, clear, cool, baby-blue sky, and happy people. Robert and Loma, my next-door neighbors, motioned for me to join them. Another friend announced he was going to bring a tray of wine for those who choose to imbibe. I was still dressed in a T-shirt, shorts, and sandals. Robert glanced across the commons to the far corner over by the memory unit's dining room and touched me on the shoulder. "Isn't that Genie over there?"

Sure enough, it was. I immediately got up and started moving toward her. As I was about halfway to her table she got up and, like a schoolgirl, skipped toward me. We met on the concrete slab just beyond the covered seating area of the commons, which was full of residents. We hugged and kissed. As we stood hugging, the all-girl high school band commissioned to play for the evening, entered from behind the covered area. Marching in a straight line, the young women paraded along the elliptical sidewalks playing swing music. Genie took my hand and said, "Let's dance." She was young again, swinging, and twisting as I turned her waist and lifted our hands above our heads for her to make a full turn. I had never seen her so radiant. Two other couples jumped up to join us. Then two or three more. Non-dancers scooted back to make more room on the concrete dance floor. It was transformative, not only for Genie and me, but for the community. Senior citizens were cutting a rug. So what if it was concrete?

When the band took a break, a couple of residents offered us their seats at the covered area. "The dancers should have the ringside seats," one of them said. We sat holding hands until the young nurse who had brought Genie and her friend Ms. Curtis to the party said it was time for them go. After a couple of kisses, Genie happily took the nurse's arm as Ms. Curtis took the other. The trio returned to the memory unit.

I did not keep count, but for that evening and two or three days that followed, many residents would stop me to say how much they enjoyed seeing us dance. Almost without exception, they would add how beautiful and graceful Genie was. Our repertoire continued to expand. I decided to take a chance and asked her to take an old hymnal down to the memory unit's activities room and play for other residents. She had not played a note for thirteen months. To my surprise, she said, "Sure." I sat beside her on the piano bench and turned the pages. She immediately picked up where she had left off, playing several of the old favorite Southern Baptist hymns: "Blessed Assurance," "Amazing Grace," "Shall We Gather at the River?" "Take My Hand Precious Lord," and that special hymn she played at the Hutchinson County Jail all those years ago, "How Great Thou Art." I had tucked another book of her favorite music under my arm. "I think they would like this one." After she played an almost flawless rendition of Rimsky-Korsakov's "Love Song of India," the residents applauded. She smiled, picked up the hymnal and book of music, took my arm, and with a spring in her step, walked with me back to her room. "That was so much fun," she said.

Just like that, playing the piano was once again an integral part of our lives. Almost every Tuesday and Thursday morning at 11:50, Monique would bring Genie to the hall where about forty residents and I were concluding a forty-five-minute session of chair Pilates. The hall has a wonderful Steinway piano in the far corner. Monique and I took turns setting it up and opening the hymnal and a book of music marked at numbers we knew Genie loved to play. She would play for about twenty minutes. Often five to ten residents would be seated in the "audience," like a Sunday morning congregation. The spectators always applauded again when I would tell Genie, "You can't leave without giving me three love kisses." She would smile, kiss me, and take Monique's hand to walk back to her room. I told myself this is a different light than the one Genie and I had basked in together for years. But it was light!

Chapter Fifty-four

Zelda was always eager to join me on my morning and afternoon walks to music time with Genie. She would start harassing me at 9:30 every morning and 4:15 every evening by wagging her tail, jumping up on her hind legs, and pawing at my leg. "Max, it's time to go see Genie and Monique." Once inside Genie's room, Zelda loved being off the lead so she could explore. I always prepared for my visit with "three shes and a he" by having small pieces of Zelda's favorite treat for Genie and Monique to hand her. Gene Alice couldn't wait to give treats to Zelda; the dog was another soul for her to love. Often by patting her hand on the seat beside her, Genie would signal to Monique or me to put Zelda beside her. She would then stroke Zelda's soft fur. Fastidious Gene Alice would even let Zelda lick her fingers. Visits with Zelda and playing the piano were so transformative I asked Monique if we should attempt what I had considered the ultimate risk, inviting Genie back to our apartment. We agreed to try.

On a Friday afternoon at 4:15, Genie and Monique came over. I had chilled a bottle of white wine, three plastic martini glasses, and a bowl of pecans. We sat on the balcony, the same balcony Genie so enjoyed with Olive. She patted the seat beside her, and I lifted Zelda onto her lap. As usual, I did all of the talking, pointing out clouds and trees and next-door-neighbor Loma's balcony garden. Genie smiled and nodded appreciatively. After about fifteen minutes she looked at Monique. "Don't you think it is time for us to go?"

It was now clear. Genie could return to the home where she had once lived with me and not protest leaving. She had her own new home with new friends, a place where she felt safe and secure. My heart treasured her coming home. My lawyer training told me how blessed we were that she could come and go. Years ago, I had witnessed families going through a living hell after taking "Mom" home, discovering the agony of not being able to be with her every minute, and struggling to adjust to the unexpected and often explosive lava coming out of the volcano of an Alzheimer's mind. I was reassured thinking that Genie and I would be able to grow old and be together until death do us part. Apart, but together.

This became our new routine. Genie and Monique joined me in the apartment almost once a week. Zelda and I formed the welcoming committee for a twenty-five-to-thirty-minute balcony party. Genie's grand piano commanded center stage in the apartment, and I didn't know if she missed playing it. It had been a part of her life since the 1960s, when she and I took the big plunge to go into debt and buy it. It had held a prominent place in our homes in Amarillo, on Greenway, and now in my apartment. I recalled that when we inspected plans for our new Westminster home, Genie asked if we could remove a wall to have a better spot for "her piano." During our three years living together at Westminster, that spot was the focal point of the room, a room where several times she played for a congregation of residents and almost daily for Olive and me. I wrestled with a major question

I couldn't answer: Should she be asked to play? Or was that too risky? Might that cause her not to want to leave the apartment?

The answer, like so many in this Alzheimer's journey, came accidentally. Betsy, our lifelong friend from Baylor and Amarillo, called to ask if she and her daughter, Jera, a skilled music teacher in Wisconsin, could stop by for a visit. As a little girl, Jera used to sit behind Genie as she practiced at the Amarillo Presbyterian church. Not only was the answer yes, but I immediately suggested that I text Monique to bring Genie to the apartment. The rendezvous was spectacular. Hugs, smiles, laughs. Jera told of being mesmerized as she watched Genie play the organ. She looked at Genie and said, "Would you play a few hymns for me?" Genie said, "I would be delighted." I found a hymnal, opened it to one that she had been playing for the residents in Harris Bell Hall. Genie enthusiastically played the first verse of "Shall We Gather at the River?" Betsy, Jera, and I joined in singing. We had a hymn fest for the next twenty minutes. Betsy sensed Genie was tiring and announced that she and Jera had to go to an appointment. Monique resolved my concern.

"Genie, why don't we walk with them?" They departed the apartment and the piano, with Genie walking happily between Betsy and Jera. All three were holding hands as I watched from the door. Encouraged, I continued to experiment and take chances. Neighbors in the eight apartments on our wing started having a random social gathering in the common area on our floor. I volunteered to bring the beverages. Others would bring pâté, nuts, and cheese. Genie, Monique, and Mary Curtis, a soon-to-be centenarian and Genie's closest friend in the memory wing, started joining us. I would leave the apartment door open — for Zelda. Her habit was to cautiously emerge and slowly start making the rounds, moving from guest to guest. Then, Genie would pat the front of her seat. Monique or I would lift Zelda onto her lap. Our third-floor family reunion would be in full swing.

The miracle of the second year of our brave new Alzheimer's world continued. I texted Monique: "Do you think she could go out for Mexican food?"

"I think so."

We decided to experiment. One Friday I picked up Genie and Monique at 11:30, the regular lunchtime for the memory unit, and off we went to Maudie's, one of our favorite haunts. I was learning to give Genie choices. I picked two of her favorites and asked which she would prefer. She picked Maudie's Plate, a regular taco and a cheese enchilada. She devoured both, showing so much pleasure, I immediately knew this would be a weekly outing.

I realize I have focused a lot on Gene Alice's serious side, but that was just one part of her. She loved letting go and acting silly. Several times, in a not-so-formal café, she would look over to me and say, "People are so quiet. No one is having fun. Let's liven it up." And then she would pucker up those wonderful lips and give a loud whistle as her four boy cousins had taught her. The other diners would be startled, but when she said, "Hey, guys, let's live it up and have some fun," most would laugh and smile as they continued eating. I often wondered whether she might one day decide to do this in a fancy formal dining room.

One day Monique was ill, and I had to attend a meeting. I did not go for my morning music session at Genie's apartment. Later, when I arrived for 11 a.m. chair Pilates, the wife of a man in the memory unit could not wait to tell me how Genie had entertained a large number of the unit's residents by just showing off and being silly. She danced a little jig and then asked one or two of the men to dance with her. "Not one of those men had the courage to take her up on her offer," the tattletale told me. I knew she was in her element.

Two days later Zelda, and I arrived for morning music several minutes early. I entered the apartment and waited for the "two shes" to return from bingo. I heard Monique whisper, "Max and Zelda are here." No one came into the room. As I looked up the narrow entry hall, Monique motioned that Genie was hiding.

"I wonder where they are?" I asked Zelda in a loud voice. "Maybe we came on the wrong day." Gene Alice's hand was slowly moving up and down along the edge of the bathroom door. She was teasing me. Gradually she pushed the door open and then gleefully pranced over to give me a hug and a kiss. This was the Genie of old. Seizing the moment, having fun like that little girl who once played hide-and-seek with her cousins. It reaffirmed my deep belief that we just needed to keep playing and having fun. We needed to keep experimenting, trying new restaurants, playing different music, finding parks for us to walk through holding hands. And by all means, we had to keep dancing.

Chapter Fifty-five

W hat is the essence of a person? Can Alzheimer's steal that away? I knew that it could rob memories and provoke new or different behaviors, but could it take away what made someone who they are? Gene Alice's favorite book was the 1972 novel, *My Name is Asher Lev*, about a young man's crisis of identity. Genie was still Genie. She cared about how she looked. Monique often told me how she would reject a certain blouse or jacket that did not match whatever she was wearing. Gene Alice's fastidious dress, her attention to detail, and her impeccable taste were the Genie I knew so well. A part of her essence.

As Zelda and I walked back to our apartment, I was thinking of the playful version of my wife and smiling to myself. I walked inside and noticed that Gene Alice Wienbroer Sherman was everywhere. She picked the paintings and the posters. She chose the frames. She picked the furniture. She determined where everything would be placed. It was her home. It was our home. Another of the homes where we had been together. She was still with me, but not in the same way. I was comforted to know that the essence of my beloved partner was intact: hugging, kissing, vibrant.

She continued playing piano for the chair-Pilates audience, and we continued meeting once a week in the Bistro to have breakfast together. I usually found a table overlooking the commons and sat with my back to the door that Monique and Genie used. Gene Alice loved to sneak up on me and give me a kiss on the head. I would always exclaim, "Where did you come from? Don't you know it's dangerous to sneak up on a fellow like that?" She would laugh. We would order blueberry pancakes, scrambled eggs, and bacon. Sitting across the table from me, she would often reach for my hand.

Things were going so well that I asked Monique if we could try going weekly to Trudy's, a restaurant Genie and I frequented for over thirty years. She said, "Let's try it." I picked them up at 10:30 on a Monday morning so we could arrive before the crowd. Monique ordered migas tacos for the two of them. I ordered the Breakfast Mexicana. Those were the same orders we had placed in years past. Often it took us a full hour or more for Genie to finish. My heart would skip a beat whenever she would reach across the table to pick up a piece of my bacon. She would wink at me, as if to say, "Didn't see me do that? Did you?"

Lunch at Southern comfort food haven Hoover's was our next experiment, only a few blocks from our old Greenway home. Before moving to Westminster, we ate there at least once a week. Her favorite dish was seared rainbow trout. If it was not on the menu that day, I would suggest the fried catfish. That was always a winner. And it did lead to choosing another favorite, the Catfish Parlour in Pflugerville. That became our destination mid-week. We worked in visits to IHOP and the Original Pancake House to add variety and new experiences. We were out on the town four days a week. I kept seizing opportunities to return to the normal life we had lived for over fifty years. I knew I was right when the care team called to say they thought it was time for me to take Genie to church.

Monique and I collaborated. She would come early on Sunday morning to help get Genie dressed. I picked her up at the building entrance at 10:30. We arrived at University Presbyterian Church much earlier than expected. Gene Alice was restless and asked, "Shouldn't we leave. No one is here." A few friends started arriving and came over to visit. It was OK. She thoroughly enjoyed the service.

The next week, Monique came again to help her dress. Monique was exhausted. Alzheimer's families too easily forget that caregivers also have lives with all the ups and downs of life. Monique had been away most of the week taking care of the details for her grandfather's funeral and spending each night at the hospital as her father recovered from a knee replacement. That morning we delayed our departure ten minutes so that we would not arrive to an empty sanctuary. On the same route we had taken for three years, Gene Alice was very much in the moment and repeated a common theme, "It is so green. The flowers are beautiful. The sun is so bright."

She identified the trees and flowers and exclaimed about their brilliant colors. She could no longer carry on a conversation, but she was naming what she saw. As we turned off of Leon Street on to Twenty-second Street to arrive at our church, Genie was quietly saying, "San Gabriel, Pearl, Rio Grande, Nueces." She was reading the street signs. She was trying to hold on to what once was so familiar.

I thought back to a time when we were newly married and read together a 1942 poem called *The Naming of Parts* by Henry Reed. It's about a new military recruit hearing the names of a rifle's parts and being distracted by a lovely springtime show of flowers. The instructor mentions cleaning the rifle, while the recruit's juxtaposed thoughts turn to the Japonica glistening like coral in the neighbors' gardens.

We were still six or eight minutes ahead of the other congregants. As we sat in our pew, I reminded her that she chaired the
committee to redesign the sanctuary. I pointed to the baptismal
font and the communion table on the raised stage. I hugged her
and whispered in her ear, "You know this is your handiwork. You
consulted with Stan Hall from the seminary and then recommended putting the baptismal font at the front of the sanctuary
— on the same level as the congregation — and the communion
table on the platform to have the congregation more intimately
involved in the worship service. You also chose the woodwork-
er to redo the front of the sanctuary and then made your most
controversial recommendation: removing a large number of pews
and angling the remaining ones to allow worshipers to come and
go more easily. Several members of the committee were reluctant
to make such a dramatic change, but, eventually, they all voted
unanimously to go along with your recommendation."

She said nothing. I went on: "You traveled the state to hear
church organs, always asking the organists to give you the pros and
cons of their instruments. That's how you made the decision to
recommend Dan Garland to build a virtually new organ."

I was pushing too hard, trying desperately to bring back the old
Genie. She politely listened but had little or no interest in her role as
chair of the sanctuary renewal and organ rebuilding committee. She
was bored. She started to fidget with her nails. She was confused.
The service was underway when she leaned over to put her head on
my shoulder. "Max, would you point to the program to let me know
where we are?" She fumbled with the hymnal trying to find the page
of the hymn the congregation was singing. She asked me to do it.
The hymn was new to us, one I knew she had never seen nor played.
Sight reading, she leaned over. "This is one of my favorite hymns,"

she said. Even though she was frustrated, she giggled when the organ bellowed a rousing rendition of "The Battle Hymn of the Republic," jabbing me in the ribs to say, "How about that!"

University Presbyterian uses a register to record attendance that gets passed around during the service. When the pad came to Genie, she took the pen and started to sign, then, with a look of frustration, handed it to me, saying, "Here, you do it." In every church service we had attended around the world, my English professor partner always signed the record of attendance.

University Presbyterian offers communion by intinction, which means dipping a piece of bread into the wine or juice before consuming. Those who are able, go forward to the altar for communion and then return to their seats. Genie and I had taken communion that way for thirty years. When it was time for our pew to go forward, she was very confused, asking me if she should take her bulletin, go forward or stay seated, even dip a finger in the font water. She took a piece of bread from our minister and immediately put it in my mouth. When she reached the elder holding the cup, she did not know what to do. I broke off a piece of my bread, took her hand, handed her the bread, and helped her dip it into the cup.

That was her last communion. Our church-going experiment lasted only for those two times. Genie's frustration with so many aspects of the service, which had been integral to her life, were my first hints that I may be expecting too much.

Over the next few weeks of fall and winter 2016, the good life we had been living began to unravel. She started dragging her feet and expressing reluctance about going to Harris Bell Hall to play the piano. When she did come, the sessions got shorter and shorter. Even sitting on the bench in front of her beloved grand piano in my apartment, she started exhibiting frustration with the music, turning pages in the hymnals when her mind was no longer processing the music. Monique and I could see the joy of playing slipping away. I did not fully understand why this was suddenly happening.

Our days of eating out started changing. Maudie's took too long, and she would get up with Monique to go for a walk after ordering. Often, they would do two or three walks before she was ready to sit down and enjoy one of her favorite meals. Hoover's and IHOP were too loud. She would rise from the table several times to take a walk. The signs that we were entering a new stage of loss from Alzheimer's came in the Bistro, at the evening meal and at breakfast the very next morning. For dinner, I brought a white wine to share. I had learned that a clink of the glass and a toast usually helped Gene Alice settle in for a forty-five-minute meal. Not so this evening. Genie frowned. She struggled to articulate her thought. "When can you...you go-go with me to see my mother? Sheee, sheee is alert. Sheee knows whh-what is go-go going on."

I had learned not to explain that her mother died almost twenty years ago. "When I get well, we will go to see your mother."

The next morning, as usual, we met for breakfast. To allow Monique time to run an errand, we sat at a table for two instead of three. Monique had barely left the room when Genie had the same frown as the evening before. She struggled to tell me, "Th-th-the night be-be-before last… I da- myself." I knew better than to inquire what it was she had done and just exclaimed, "Oh, really." She started to get up. I knew that she was not going to wait for the meal to be served. I said, "Let me text Monique. She will be here in a minute." She rubbed her eyes, a new and frequent habit, and lamented, "I am so tired."

I was terrified, but I knew her increasing frustrations were a signal that she was moving more rapidly into a more acute stage of

Alzheimer's. Forty-five minutes was now too long to sit at a table with me. I immediately texted Monique to alert her to return as soon as possible. That was our last breakfast in the Bistro.

Our son, Lynn, and I agreed to meet Genie in the Bistro on Father's Day. When Genie and Monique arrived through the commons, Genie gave each of us a big hug. We took turns telling her how beautiful she was and how much we liked her hair. Still, she was pensive, staring out into the commons and, in a reflective tone, mentioned the beautiful flowers and bright sun. She reached over to take our hands and spoke haltingly, but we got the message. "I am so excited to be here with my two men. I want to tell you about this wonderful place I found. It is a lovely room on a corner. I did it all by myself." I remembered the times over the years when she proudly recounted times when she "did it all by myself." Finding an apartment in Texas City. Tracking down an apartment at Evangeline House in New York. Convincing Ms. Ihlenfeld to rent her a room in Madison. The "wonderful place" she was telling us about was the same room she referred to as "this little place where I am." Tears crept down my cheek as I remembered her plea in those first days, "You have to come and get me. I shouldn't be here. This is not my home."

Fortunately, I had learned that laughter would sometimes bring her back. "You've been that way all of your life, finding a place to rally the troops, especially the men. They will all have to meet in your corner room." She did not bring it up again.

The following month, our daughter and our son, along with their families, took Genie and me to celebrate the Fourth of July at the Hillside Farmacy, a popular and funky Austin restaurant. Nine members of our immediate family had a rollicking morning telling stories that elicited hearty belly laughs. Our six granddaughters saw Genie smile, laugh, and several times say, "Oh, pshaw, did that really happen?"

Afterward, Holly and her husband, Carlos, dropped me off at my apartment. Lynn took Genie to her room. I sat down to read the Sunday morning newspaper. The main story in the *Parade* magazine insert was on Alzheimer's. It pointed out the following: The disease is rising. Every sixty-seven seconds someone in the United States develops it. An estimated 5.3 million Americans have it, and one in three seniors will die of Alzheimer's or some other form of dementia. It is the sixth leading cause of death, and, most startling, it is the only cause of death in the top ten in America that cannot be treated, cured, or slowed. Maria Shriver was quoted. "Today nearly two-thirds of those with Alzheimer's are women and more than 70 percent of Alzheimer's caregivers are women. Women are the epicenter of this crisis," she said.

A section on the unmet needs of those suffering with Alzheimer's spoke of their need to be included and the importance of confronting the disease's stigma. I had just read about the need for caregivers to focus on the quality of life by understanding the basics of the disease so that they could communicate in a kinder, more effective way. I was jerked away from my reading when my phone rang. It was Genie, using the cellphone Holly had found for her. "You have to come and get me. I'm ready to come home. I am down here and ready to go. I can get my things together."

I could easily hear the desperation in her voice. It was a Sunday; Monique was not there. Her family was not there. She did not remember how much fun she had just had at the Hillside Farmacy. I realized she was simply bored.

Chapter Fifty-six

The good life of the last few months was quickly disappearing. I was torn. My rational intellect and lawyer training told me to deal with the reality of the situation. Follow the facts and the best medical advice you can get. Alzheimer's is a progressive disease. There is no cure. There will be ups and downs, good days and bad. But I knew the overall trajectory was down. She will not ever return to being the Genie you married, your wise and constant companion. That life is gone forever. The lover, husband, and partner cried inside and wished to deny that truth.

I was fragile and grieving. I watched *The Water Diviner*, a movie with Russell Crowe as a father who went to Gallipoli to find the bodies of his three sons killed in that World War I slaughter. The young boy who becomes almost a surrogate son takes him on a tour of Istanbul afterward. They are in the stunning Blue Mosque. As Crowe's character looks up at the unbelievably gorgeous art on the ceiling, I gasp and blurt out a sob from some long-suppressed emotion. It conjured a memory, and I could not stop sobbing. In 1999, my Christmas gift to Gene Alice was a trip to Turkey. I had made reservations at the luxury Four Seasons Hotel at Sultanahmet, the center of Old Istanbul. The hotel site was a former prison and I had lined up a Texan to guide us through the historic city. She called herself the Shopper Lady and was a friend of friends, but we never met her.

You may recall that the world was going crazy over "Y2K." Computers reportedly were not prepared to make the transition from one century to the next, which would cause a catastrophic breakdown of electricity and communications. Airline traffic control systems would go on the blink, planes would crash, disaster was afoot. Americans had constructed underground bunkers as hide-outs. Our family and friends kept protesting, "You cannot be flying across the world in December of 1999 and January 2000. You just can't run the risk of crashing in the ocean." For the longest time, I resisted their warnings but finally surrendered and canceled all of our reservations. I still had a letter from the manager of the Four Seasons who was understanding and gave us a guaranteed free week whenever we made it to Istanbul. We never did. "Oh, Genie, I'm sorry," I said through my sobs. She would have loved being there.

But memories can cut both ways. Two helped sustain me as I moved into what for me was the third world of Alzheimer's. Genie and I had labored through months of living with the possibility that the disease would abruptly worsen, like a fall from a cliff.

We once went to a buffalo jump in Montana, a place where Native American hunters had driven herds of buffalo over a cliff. The jumps would occur early in the morning when young braves would go out to round-up the herd, nudging strays into the main grazing pasture until a large number were gathered together. The stampede would start when the brave in charge shot a flaming arrow into the air. Other braves had strategically placed piles of brush around the perimeter of the herd and then ignited them, leaving the cliff as the only escape. As the frightened, shaggy creatures picked up speed, there would be no turning back. They would tumble over the precipice landing on top of each other, breaking necks, wailing with broken legs and ribs. The rest of the tribe would be waiting below in case spears and bows were needed to finish them off. Gene Alice and I saw photos of the bones and rubble of those ancient graveyards. We hiked down and walked among the remains. We were struck by the sadness of that place.

When Genie and I returned to our home on the Yellowstone River, she googled "buffalo jump" to help us learn more. The Native Americans used the bison for food, clothing, and shelter. Plains Indians in particular depended on them for their survival. Every part of the animal was used in some way: hides for clothes and shelter, bones for tools, sinews for bowstrings and laces. Hooves could be ground for glue, and the brains could be used in the tanning process for the hides. The extra meat was preserved as food for the winter. We sat on the deck for one of our wonderful times together discussing our thoughts on the walk through the remains of lives played out hundreds of years before ours. I never forgot what she said. "I guess you just have to be willing to rummage through the rubble." She was right. The relics of our long life together often brought me comfort.

The second memory was another succinct bit of wisdom from Gene Alice after I was invited to represent Westminster residents on a podcast with sixteen senior living facilities around the country. Each team was represented by the head of nursing, the activities director, the director of social services, and a representative of the residents. I had taken a sixteen-week, forty-eight-hour crash course on dementia and Alzheimer's. Because of that intensive training, I was asked to write an article in the Westminster newsletter to drum up support for the annual Texas Walk to End Alzheimer's. I ended the article by advising readers to "be in the moment, treasure the moment. Just because it worked today doesn't mean it will work tomorrow. You may not be able to capture the same happy moment that you had yesterday. If you see it's not working, change it, move on, and try something else. There are happy times to be had. …There is light at the end of the tunnel…it's just not the same light you knew before."

I was perplexed about what do with what I had learned from my cram course on Alzheimer's. In my mind's eye, Genie and I were having a conversation just as we had done almost daily since our first root beer date at Baylor. I could hear her saying, "Follow your own advice, Max." I knew that was what I had to do.

Chapter Fifty-seven

Our trek through the third world of Alzheimer's was familiar but different. It was like we were dating again, getting to know each other once more. Gene Alice would tease me, much like that gorilla at the Broadmoor zoo had once singled me out for a laugh. She would jab me in the ribs as if to ask, "Didn't know I could do that, did you?" She would giggle when I kissed her on the ear. Kiss after kiss, she would giggle. She would laugh when I rubbed her neck. And, my favorite, she would duck her head pretending to be asleep, but laugh impishly at some crazy thing I would say or if I would reach over and tickle her under the chin. It was like she was filling her cheeks with water waiting for the propitious moment to squirt it in my face. I was happy that she still had her sense of humor. The essence of Gene Alice shined through.

In those early days when we were getting to know each other as newlyweds, we dined two evenings in the five-star Broadmoor Penrose Room, listening to soothing music from a live string quartet. In our Alzheimer's world, we dined at the Dairy Queen in Austin with steak fingers, French fries, and gravy, listening to country western music over the loudspeaker. Or, we would go upscale to La Pâtisserie in Pflugerville for strawberry crepes, croissants, and French hot chocolate where the owner is concierge, waiter, and cook. There was no music. If it was raining or if Genie was tired, we would gamble on Trudy's and hope it would be fast. Otherwise, Monique would go with her for a three- or four-minute walk under the awning.

When a granddaughter would visit, we would return to the Bistro, knowing Genie and Monique would take a walk or two and rarely stay with us for long. As Genie and Monique would take their leave, Gene Alice usually would stand beside her granddaughter, reach down to hold her face, and smile to say, "I love you." The loving person Genie had always been remained.

In this new world, we could still meet on the second- or third-floor balconies at Westminster and sit, hip to hip, and take turns leaning a head onto the other's shoulder. I would sneak up on her with ear kisses, which always got a hearty laugh. Almost every weekday afternoon, she and Monique would join me in the apartment. If the weather allowed, we would sit on the balcony. If not, Genie would sit in her recliner, hold my hand across the table between us, and drink the non-alcoholic beer I handed her. She would not play the piano, and I had learned not to suggest it. It had become too frustrating for her to sit at the bench with a familiar hymnal in front of her and not know what to do.

She had stopped trying to cut my hair. Instead, she would stand with her hand on my shoulder while Monique trimmed my much too-long hair, watching, as if inspecting to see whether Monique's work measured up to her own, in better years. If the hair trim met her satisfaction, she would wander from room to room as if checking out my housekeeping.

There was light; it just was not the same light we once knew.

Chapter Fifty-eight

Life with Gene Alice was different, but we still shared moments of sheer pleasure. I looked for ways to celebrate life, with Genie beside me. I vowed not to miss any opportunities and jumped at the chance when Malissa, the memory unit's weekend nurse, called me on a Saturday early in the summer of 2019. "Mr. Sherman, would you be able to come over to the Memory Care Garden just outside the dining room to sit with Ms. Sherman and have a glass of wine?" she asked. "I am trying an experiment to get residents out for Saturday and Sunday evenings. I think it would help if you are here." I was there ten minutes ahead of the 6:30 rendezvous. Malissa and Genie held hands as they made their way from the dining room. I met them at the door. Genie and I shared a rocker loveseat. We snuggled up close. She leaned her head on my shoulder. I leaned over to kiss her ear. She laughed and flashed her infectious smile. We were making love as we had learned to do since the Alzheimer's tsunami.

Several women joined us. Health aides formed a tight-knit circle of wheelchairs and walkers. Mary and Ann, two of the three more mobile women, sat in the other loveseat directly across from us and rocked slowly back and forth. We each had a small glass of wine. Mary, who was soon to be a hundred years old, took charge and led us in singing "The Eyes of Texas." After "'til Gabriel blows his horn" she said, "Let's sing it again." Over and over we sang "The Eyes of Texas," the same verse, over and over.

When Ann had had enough, she pointed to Genie. "Is that your girlfriend or your wife?"

"She is my wife."

"Where did you meet her?"

"We met in jail."

Ann was incredulous. "Oh, that can't be true. Tell us about it."

The women perked up. I knew that these women with Alzheimer's and dementia would not be able to follow a long-winded story, so I gave an abbreviated version.

"I was one of four high school boys who held a church service each Sunday afternoon at the Hutchinson County Jail. We invited an all-boy quartet to come and sing. One Sunday, they brought a beautiful young girl to accompany them on an old army fold-up field organ. As she was unfolding it, I saw her elegant ankles and said to myself, 'I'm going to marry that girl.' And eight years later, I did." The audience of women with dementia applauded and in unison urged me on. "Tell it again. Tell it again."

For several Saturday and Sunday evenings this was the routine: Sing "The Eyes of Texas" several times and recite the jail story several times. The women never seemed to tire of it, but I did. One evening when Ann goaded me, "Tell how you met that girl," I made up a story.

"One day I was riding my pony across the plains and came upon a tepee village. As I got closer, this stunningly beautiful girl popped out of one without a stitch of clothes on. She jumped on a white stallion and started riding across the plains. I said, 'By gum, I'm going to catch her.'"

The women burst out laughing, even those in wheelchairs who seldom raised their heads. Several of the ones who barely speak joined the chorus, "Tell us about the tepees."

I had become the grand storyteller. Ann kept baiting me. "Tell more. There has to be more. What happened next? When did you see her again? Did she ever know you were watching her?"

I hesitated to tell what might be considered an off-color story to a group of older, probably conservative women. But then I remembered the most important woman in Genie's life, her mother Tavia, the daughter of a Baptist minister, would laugh uproariously at a dirty joke. I decided that most of the women in the memory garden audience were cut from that same cloth. They would never admit it, but they, too, loved a risqué story. I rose to the occasion with an even more daring story of the young girl in the tepee. I told them that I followed her and snuck up on a hill to watch her bathe in a spring. Ann was satisfied. The women did not laugh, but smiled approvingly.

Chapter Fifty-nine

I was basking in good feelings about our new normal when the wheels came off. The whole world was fighting a global pandemic against what the president of the United States called "the evil enemy," a new virus that was mystifying, even to scientists. Nursing homes and senior living communities were considered the primary targets of the new virus as it preyed on older people, especially those with health vulnerabilities. Westminster was on lockdown and early on reported that a staff member had been infected. Loved ones could not visit in the health and memory care units. It was simply too risky, with so many fragile residents.

Most family members of loved ones with Alzheimer's never have to face anything like this, and I immediately realized what it meant. Time together is over for the foreseeable future. It's an undiscovered territory for me and Gene Alice, and I have to try and forge a path forward. I can't allow grief or anger at circumstances beyond our control to overwhelm me, but it's hard to avoid those emotions.

I have not seen Genie for months. I terribly miss kissing her ear and resting my head on her shoulder. These precious moments when Genie still knows who I am and knows we love each other are evaporating, day by day. And my fears are mounting. The worst is: I will never see her again. Although we are both in good health, our age puts us in the high-risk group of dying from a COVID-19 infection. The hell of Alzheimer's does not compare to the hell of the virus. At least before, we could see each other. Now residents are staying behind closed doors, in their apartments. I have groceries delivered. Occasionally, I cook. The Bistro is closed; activities have been shut down. I call Genie, and we do FaceTime once or twice a week. I think she knows me, but what Alzheimer's can do scares me. The thought that she or I might die without holding the other is my greatest worry. I know that if Genie, my senior partner, my editor, my closest friend, the love of my life, were operating at full throttle right now, she would chastise me. "Don't throw in the towel. End with resurrection. End with trust. End with hope," she would say.

She would be pleased that I use a phrase from the boxing ring because confronting Alzheimer's is the fight of one's life. The lover and the beloved must put on boxing gloves. There will be blows to the face and below the belt. There will be cut lips and blood and swollen eyes. There will be times when the caregiver collapses to the ground and screams, "Enough!"

I picture Genie in her small room. Her first-floor space is in a separate wing of the complex and has two large windows that meet in the middle, one facing east and the other facing north. In my mind's eye, I see Genie watching the bird feeder that dangles in front of her east window and brings pleasure to her world. She mentioned it to me many times, when she was still able to talk.

"I can look those birds right in the eye," she would tell me.

Gene Alice Wienbroer Sherman is looking me straight in the eye, and she has something important to say. "Don't throw in the damn towel. End the Alzheimer's boxing match with my hand raised above my head, a woman, the victor, the Muhammad Ali of the battle with Alzheimer's. There is no knockout. I win by scoring more points, putting up a good fight, one step at a time."

And how she scored points. I watched Genie, with her strong sense of self, independence, and determination over the years. When she felt strongly about something, she could roar like a lion, and I don't mean a ferocious lion looking to intimidate or tear apart a weaker rival. It was a roar of conviction. The smoldering core inside Genie, the lion with Alzheimer's, is the partner who would say:

"I can do it myself."

"I was your editor when you were named one of thirty finalists for the White House Fellows program."

"I campaigned with you across a vast West Texas senate district until we were almost too tired to undress before falling into bed."

"I was your sounding board, confidante, and adviser when you were in the senate."

"I helped craft your inaugural remarks when you became a university president."

"I am your partner in all things 'until death do us part.'"

Not only did Genie score points as a pugilist, she scored as a scholar. Lynn discovered a treasure in a box she packed for Westminster. It was a paper about twins Genie gave to an Austin club of university and professional women, Open Forum. Of course, she was interested in twins, having two sets of identical twin granddaughters *in the same family.* She delivered the remarks not long after her first visit to the Center on BrainHealth in Dallas.

Now, with Genie in her time of Alzheimer's, I read the words she wrote with new meaning: "Recently I had an experience with the three-year-old granddaughters, Clara and Hasie, that I hope I will never forget," she told the Open Forum. "At my house one afternoon, they wanted to look at my albums of family photographs. I said 'OK,' thinking, 'This won't last long,' and I brought out one album, then at their request, another and another. We spent three hours on the breakfast room couch, three hours, with only one break for ice cream, looking at these books of family photos. And over and over came the question, 'Where is me?' 'Where is me?'

"Pretty soon in that three hours, they could identify grandparents, great-grandparents, cousins, godparents, and other friends, but there was always their most important concern, 'Where is me?' I did my best to point out who was Hasie and who was Clara, whenever either appeared in a photograph. Their images looking so much alike, I often had to check the label on the back to be sure, and they insisted that I do so.

"I hope I never forget that day because it is such a clear reminder of how these little ones come into the world as unique persons and develop so very soon an incredibly strong sense of identity and individual personality that deserves respect from everyone."

In this moment, she telegraphed to me and to the world that every single person struggling with dementia and Alzheimer's is unique, with a strong personality and sense of self. In myriad ways, every day, those strong personalities with Alzheimer's cry out, "Where is me?"

Gene Alice is in a corner room looking the birds straight in the eye.

She is sketching and painting.

She is singing hymns from memory.

She is whistling.

She is hugging her helpers.

She is smiling.

She is hugging my neck as I kiss her ear.

She is laughing.

I hold her hand above her head to say, "You sure as hell won that round."

And so, as we live in this world of COVID-19, "Where is Genie?" She is in my memory and my heart and, whenever possible, on FaceTime. I have come to accept that I may never be in the same room with her again.

Alone in my apartment, I have found I can switch dark moods into happy ones by looking at our trove of photographs. I have more than a thousand pictures of Genie. She is canoeing, skiing, fishing, meeting royalty, conversing with governors, playing piano at parties, surrounded by friends, extending her hand to greet a president, singing, playing the organ for a church service, chatting happily with spouses of elected officials, speaking to a group. I see her in Montana standing beside the Yellowstone River or Fairy Lake, surrounded by beauty — the Big Sky, the rushing water, the ring of mountains. Her gaze reflects back the beauty and serenity, and I note those same attributes are central to her essence. I see photos of her leading twenty or thirty senior citizens from a Thompson Conference Center educational travel program to England, Scotland, and France where she tended to their every need. I find photos of her as a mother from years earlier and realize she exudes the same nurturing and confident look. In one photo, she is a new mother with a tiny infant in her arms and then walking hand-in-hand with our son and daughter when they were small. Later, she is sitting on the floor, playing with her children's children.

In every scene, I notice she was always exquisitely dressed and always appropriate for the occasion. That's not a surprise, just a reminder of who she is and how she lived.

Sometimes, I sit quietly alone with my thoughts. Occasionally, they drift back to the BrainHealth center and Dr. John Hart's amazement at Gene Alice's responses to his probing questions about her life. Today, I imagine myself being the one in the hot seat, with Dr. Hart, surrounded by interns, asking me the same questions he asked Genie. "Look back over your life with Ms. Sherman and tell me one of your favorite memories," he commands.

I flash back to what I consider the seminal event of our lives. The story I wrote for my final project in theater class at Baylor, the one about the brave and the butterfly. Gene Alice would always beg me to tell the story, and when I did, I would see tears in her eyes. She confessed that she identified with the butterfly because the one thing she wanted most was her freedom. To stretch her wings and fly. I wanted her with me every moment before she was ready to commit to the Partnership. She later confessed that my story was the reason she twice declined my marriage proposal. It was also the foundation for her eventually saying yes. But first, I had to release her, like the brave in my story. And I had to wait until she was ready. Genie assured me that she chose me for the right reason: love.

In my mind, I can hear Gene Alice saying now, "Max, I am free. You are free. In this crazy world of Alzheimer's, COVID-19, and isolation, we can still fly freely. Let's hold hands. Let's hug. Let's kiss. Laugh when I wiggle my nose. I want to snuggle up close to you in a chair or on my bed. I love you, and I know you love me. What more could a girl want?"

In my journey with Gene Alice and Alzheimer's, many times she would ask me to "wait" if I moved too fast or pushed her too hard. I realize I was blinded to a truth many years before when I proposed marriage twice to Genie and twice she said to wait. I foolishly took her response as a rejection of me. I realize now it wasn't about me; it was about her. Her "wait" was an invitation to do just that. Wait. What was she waiting for? She was waiting to be Genie. She instinctively knew we both had growing up to do, and she needed to know who she was.

I'm back in Dr. Hart's office. He leans in closely and speaks gently. "Tell me about your favorite memory from the world of politics."

Is this a trick question, I wonder, because I have many great memories. Being elected the first time to the state senate. Serving in the honorary role of "governor for a day." Campaigning with Gene Alice. I stop there because I know — and she must have known — she would have made a great senator. If only the times and our conservative senate district had been more welcoming to women candidates. I can't help but tell Dr. Hart about the speech Genie gave in 1988 for the Distinguished Women's Service Awards, sponsored by a group she helped found in 1976. She urged more women to get involved in politics, saying that women would make the world a more equal and better place. Gene Alice made the world better, I tell Dr. Hart.

He nods and tells me he has one last question. "I will never get to interview you and Ms. Sherman again so tell me, how will you remember her?"

This one is easy. It is the blend of beauty, music, and intelligence. I recall for him our trip to Israel and the Mahler performance by the Israel Philharmonic Orchestra. There is not an empty seat in the house. We are part of the US delegation that includes politicians at all levels of government. We are the guests of honor and are seated in the first two rows, just below the conductor. Genie and I are in the two end seats on the right aisle of the second row. At the intermission, we scatter to restrooms, men out the door to the left, women to the right. The lights are dimming to start the second half of the concert, and Genie is still gone. I know the women's room, whenever we go to a big event, is always packed. Gene Alice rushes back toward the auditorium door, which closes seconds before she reaches it.

"When I arrived at the door at the right front of the auditorium, a young Israeli soldier stepped in front of me and lifted his AK-47 across his chest to block the entrance," she told me later. "I looked him straight in the eye and confidently said, 'It is important that I get to my seat.' He didn't know whether to shoot me or let me in. He opened the door."

Zubin Mehta, the thirty-nine-year-old conductor, is poised, like Batman over Gotham, with his baton raised to strike the first note of Gustav Mahler's Symphony No. 2 (Resurrection). At that very moment, he must have noticed the door hurriedly open and a woman walking. He watches a stunning thirty-seven-year-old blonde glide down the aisle, unabashed and unhurried, to take her seat. Beside me. Mehta then lowers his baton, turns graciously to allow the elegant, golden-gowned beauty to be seated. He then returns the baton to its poised position, and music fills the hall. I am convinced I saw him and Genie nod to each other. And there were whispers from the audience.

"Who is that?"

"Is she a Scandinavian princess?"

"Could she be the wife of one of the governors?"

Gene Alice Wienbroer Sherman knew exactly who she was. Always has.

Afterword

I did not set out to write a self-help book about coping with a spouse who has Alzheimer's disease. But in writing this book about my journey with my beloved Gene Alice, I helped myself. I came to see that while similarities abound, every Alzheimer's journey is different. I claim no deep insight into how others must come to terms with a dementia or Alzheimer's diagnosis, but I gained insight into my own struggle to not only survive but be happy.

Writing about my life with Genie has been painful, joyful, and healing. I have learned a lot about us — our relationship and its nuances — and more about Alzheimer's than I ever wanted to know. I realize now that my flashes of anger at Gene Alice's insistence that we stop doing a certain activity we had long enjoyed were cries for help, from both of us. Genie wanted to control whatever part of her life she still could as much as I wanted us to continue being the couple we had always been. My identity was tied to the person I was throughout our relationship; Gene Alice's identity was evolving. I needed to change along with her, but acceptance is a long and twisty road with detours that can make the traveler feel lost and angry all over again.

This memoir was my attempt to pay tribute to my greatest love and to tell our story. Gene Alice and I virtually grew up together.

We married for love. Our life has been a thrill and a joy. I wanted to end on one of my happiest memories of her because I realize I must look at the totality of our lives together and not just the last few years. I can't imagine that the Partnership could have been a happier one than one we've had. I could not have had a more caring, generous, and loving partner. I feel like Lou Gehrig standing before a huge crowd, acknowledging that while there is pain in my life, I consider myself, in Gehrig's words, "the luckiest man on the face of this earth." I could not have been luckier than to marry Gene Alice.

The other purpose I had in writing about our journey with Alzheimer's was to give those in the same boat a life jacket. An Alzheimer's diagnosis does not require a move to Bleak House. We decided to continue to live our lives as fully and as happily as possible. Most of that fell to me because I know best what Genie loves. I've had to learn, through trial and error, how to continue to feed those passions, sometimes in new and different ways. Alzheimer's changes the lives of individuals affected and their loved ones, but it does not end the possibility of experiencing connection and joy. Most significantly, love endures. Gene Alice and I still have that, despite the disease.

In writing about the events in this memoir, I've tried to be as precise as possible, quoting from letters, notes, and other sources whenever possible. Scenes and dialogue have been reconstructed to the best of my ability, but at eighty-five, my memory is not perfect. I've also changed a few names.

The COVID-19 pandemic has injected a whole new layer of complication and uncertainty into our story. As I noted earlier, it has been months since I've been permitted to see Gene Alice, although we do FaceTime about once a week. I do the talking, and she reacts with widened eyes and smiles. She is always exquisitely dressed, usually walking, and I love that she pulls up close to the phone Monique, her caregiver, is holding to try to see me and hear my voice.

I don't know how our story ends. Act V hasn't been written, and the final curtain has yet to fall. But I can't dwell on endings. Our fifty-ninth wedding anniversary came July 29, 2020, marking the start of a new year for the Partnership. Alzheimer's has taught me to dwell in the moment, and I try to do that until memories carry me off. When they do, Gene Alice and I are together. We are holding hands, whispering to each other. I am kissing her ear. Genie is laughing. She is free.

Acknowledgements

First and foremost, I thank my wife, Gene Alice, for all of her contributions to this book. She remains my best friend, my biggest cheerleader, and my lifelong inspiration. She made sacrifices throughout our seven decades together and is the reason for any successes I have had. She is the most amazing partner anyone could want and embodies the meaning of love. She helped with this memoir in multiple ways: She kept a trove of writings in her journals, letters, and speeches. When she was able, she helped me resurrect facts I had buried. I could never thank her enough.

Before I thank the many friends who helped with this book, I must express my deep gratitude to Mary Ann Roser, my editor. She brought her careful eye and hand to polish a 10,000-piece jigsaw puzzle and shape it into this manuscript. To her, I am eternally grateful.

Dear friends of ours, some of them lifelong, who understood the tumult of Alzheimer's that Gene Alice and I were going through came to my aid as I journeyed through various iterations of this book. It started as a form of therapy to help me cope with my grief. My goal was always to celebrate Gene Alice and our love for each other. I initially envisioned writing a play with Gene Alice as Emily and me as George, the stage manager and therapist. My inspiration was Thornton Wilder's *Our Town*. A three-act play morphed into five acts. These friends read all or part of what I was writing, often into the wee hours, and encouraged me to keep pushing forward, including Joanne James, Jan Williams, Marilyn Duncan, Laura Wilson, Bill Moyers, Susan Beresford, Kathryn Meador Thomason, Nancy Tardy, Hamilton Beasley, Andy Rich, Terry Babcock-Lumish, Marvin Knox, Marv Knox (Marvin's son), Leah Tunnell, Diana Wienbroer, Joanna Hitchcock, Suzanne Wofford, Rich Oppel, Betsy Singleton, and Lee Hinson-Hasty.

I cannot thank enough the staff at Westminster Manor for keeping me and Genie safe, especially Monique Guzman, Gene Alice's daily companion and a true heaven-sent angel. Monique was indispensable in helping me reconstruct key dates during Gene Alice's time in memory care.

Finally, I am deeply grateful to our children, Lynn and Holly, whose love and support were invaluable. They gave advice, feedback, and most importantly, they always encouraged me by saying, "Keep going, Dad."

Made in the USA
Middletown, DE
05 November 2020